Santa Claus

COLLECTION

Dana Wade's collection of Paul Gordon's whimsical gourd-head characters puts all manner of vintage trims on display.

Photograph by Ed Gohlich

Volume 5

Better Homes and Gardens® Creative Collection™
Des Moines, Iowa

Holiday Dreamin'

Allow yourself to dream this holiday season of peace and goodwill to all. Envision the joy you can bring to family and friends. Then focus your aspirations on doing whatever you can to spread the joy of the season.

To do that, prepare to celebrate this Christmas season in the spirit of the kindliest of gentlemen—Santa Claus himself. His legendary presence lives on in those who share in his beliefs and who give of themselves to bring hope and delight to others.

Savor our *Santa Claus Collection, Volume 5* this holiday season and for years to come, and share the beautiful photos and inspiring stories with your family and friends. Whether you're a collector, an artisan, or simply a holiday-lover, we know you'll appreciate the harbingers of the season we've gathered together in the pages of this book and the ideas that will help you spread your own brand of Christmas cheer.

And we hope that, ultimately, you'll be inspired to join the ranks of Santa's helpers. Gather ideas to bedeck your home, and then generously open wide your door to others; choose holiday gifts to seek out from our master crafters or to make yourself; and put together a wish list of treasures you'd love to add to your own Santa collection for Christmases to come.

And remember, at this magical time of year, it really is possible for all your special holiday hopes and dreams to come true.

Believe!

Photographs by Ed Gohlich

A MERRY CHRISTMAS AND HAPPY NEW YEAR

Table of
Contents

Opposite: *Artist Lois Clarkson's Santas almost seem to come to life, bringing with them the spirit of a magical season.*

Photograph by Perry Struse

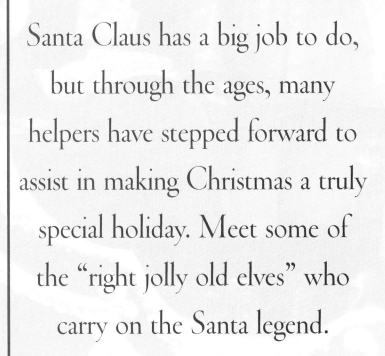

LASTING LEGENDS

Santa Claus has a big job to do, but through the ages, many helpers have stepped forward to assist in making Christmas a truly special holiday. Meet some of the "right jolly old elves" who carry on the Santa legend.

Winter scenes, elaborate sets, and very-real-looking reindeer all made the magic of Santa come alive for hundreds of children at Marshall Field's department stores.

The Store will be closed all day
Monday, December 26

Santa Claus
will travel
12,000 miles
in Marshall
Field & Company
delivery trucks today,
a distance nearly equal
to one-half way around
the world, and *he will
not be late.* ♣♣♣ Any
gift selected by six
o'clock tonight will be
delivered "in time for
Christmas." Deliveries
will cover our entire
regular city
and subur-
ban districts
after the
closing hour.

**MARSHALL FIELD
& COMPANY**

Above: *A newspaper advertisement of December 23, 1901, guarantees that Marshall Field & Company delivery drivers will not disappoint the children of last-minute gift givers.*

Opposite: *In December 1937, a young Jack Jones of Rantoul, Illinois, shared his Christmas wishes with Marshall Field's Santa Claus.*

Santa Goes Retail

FROM MACY'S TO MARSHALL FIELD'S, THE DEPARTMENT-STORE SANTA HAS BECOME A HOLIDAY SEASON STAPLE.

As the notion of Santa Claus embraced America, gift giving grew as part of the legend and department stores naturally joined in the merrymaking. By the mid-1800s, retailers nationwide had begun selling ornaments and holiday wares and dreaming up new ways to build demand. How could they entice customers to their stores? They found the answer in Santa Claus, who delivered sacks of holiday excitement in traditions that remain intact to this day.

Most people recognize Macy's Department Store in New York City as the nation's first "official Santa headquarters," where Santa appeared in 1862, just four years after the store opened at Sixth Avenue and 14th Street. A year prior, owner R. H. Macy ran a newspaper ad purporting that the jolly old man had dropped off

Written by Judith Stern Friedman ✦ *Photographs courtesy of Macy's and Marshall Field's*

gifts at Macy's, and people flocked there in hopes of catching a glimpse. The following year, Santa stayed to welcome them, shaking the hands of countless dreamers, and greeting the gazes of bewildered children. Inspired by his best friend and circus genius P. T. Barnum, Macy had laid the groundwork for a New York Christmas tradition that would continue for generations to come.

According to Bob Rutan, Macy's archivist and Director of Event Operations, "Since 1862, there has never been a time that Santa has not been at Macy's during the holiday season." Originally, he simply strolled around the store, and by 1915, Macy's had dedicated floor space for a visiting area. Festive wall murals, twinkling trees, and curious elves combined to create a different theme every year. Scenes like Toy

Land and a pirate's Adventure Land led imaginations down fantasy paths, but the end was always the highlight of the tour, where Santa sat patiently waiting on his throne. In exchange for children's whispered secret wishes, he offered souvenirs, such as puzzles, flip cards, and other treasures that even included the comic book, "Santa Meets Superman."

SEEING IS BELIEVING

Macy's may have popularized retail's holiday connection, but it certainly wasn't the only—or even the first—stop on Santa's route. As consumerism took flight, so did Claus and his magical entourage, landing in department stores all over America. In 1841, shoppers at J.W. Parkinson's in Philadelphia were among the first to witness "Criscringle" come down the chimney above the store entrance. At The Boston Store in Brockton, Massachusetts, parents and their children chugged by train from as far as Providence, Rhode Island, to whisper their hopes to the real Santa. For days, people waited in long lines outside the store for a chance to live out their Christmas fantasies.

Meanwhile, Chicago's Marshall Field's was establishing Midwest traditions. Tony Jahn, Marshall Field's historian, says, "We did Christmastime in a really big way." In the 1880s, general manager Harry Gordon Selfridge felt it was important that retail draw attention. "It was about as much color as possible," Jahn explains, "with lights, garlands, and mistletoe

At Macy's, Santa's listening ear has been poised for Christmas wishes since 1862. The tradition has grown around him, and Santa Land now employs more than two hundred workers.

Opposite: Santa's cozy throne still sits in the middle of a cottage scene built in Marshall Field's department store in 1948. His elaborate surroundings enhance the atmosphere but also serve as a diversion for children during their long wait to sit on his lap.

throughout the building." People came from all over
to admire the extravagant holiday show, which of
course included Santa Claus. Advertisements spread
word of Santa's timely deliveries, while box covers
promoted the "Store of the Christmas Spirit."

Keeping pace with the period's lavish decorating
style, in the 1870s department stores also began
trimming storefront windows, creating more elaborate
scenes each year. Mechanical dolls first appeared in
the 1880s, their splendid Victorian costumes and
animated expressions adding a human element. Macy's
credits designer Tony Sarg, noted children's writer,
illustrator, and puppeteer, for its windows from 1918
through the late 1930s. His window scenes attracted so
many lingering admirers that the city had to block off
traffic on the street. (At that time, the Christmas
windows lined 34th Street; in 1964, they moved to the
Broadway/Herald Square side where the light was
more flattering to color television broadcasts.)

STRIKE UP THE BAND

The holiday fanfare grew in 1924, when Macy's staged
its first holiday parade under management by three
brothers—Herbert, Jessie, and Percy Strauss. Rutan
says the idea came from Macy's employees, first- and
second-generation European immigrants whose
traditions were rooted in public celebrations. Kicking
off on Thanksgiving Day, the parade was to end at
Herald Square. Santa ushered in the grand finale
when he raised his hand to unveil the windows. "The
parade made Macy's Santa the big guy," Rutan says.

"They knew from the start this would be a tradition,"
Rutan adds. After the 1924 parade, the store advertised
in six newspapers its promise to hold a parade every
year thereafter. World War II (1942–1944) was the only
period when it was not held due to gas rationing and a
shortage of rubber that was needed for the balloons.

Rutan admits that the Macy's Thanksgiving Day
Parade wasn't the first of its kind. "People didn't have
TV or radio," he explains. "Parades celebrating the

*Dating back to the early nineteenth century, parades were a
common vehicle for American celebrations. Other than its
revocation during World War II, only two times was Macy's
Thanksgiving Day Parade almost canceled—upon JFK's
assassination and after 9/11—but each time the President
requested that the show go on.*

Opposite: *As part of their visit to see Santa Claus in the
1940s, children strolled with their parents down the aisles of
Marshall Field's fourth-floor toy department.*

holidays were very common back then." Peoria, Illinois, claims to have held the first Santa Claus Parade in 1889, which commemorated the opening of a new bridge over the Illinois River. Shipper and Block (later Block & Kuhl) department store sponsored the procession in which Santa Claus arrived via coach and six black horses. By the early 1900s, he came by train, was escorted through downtown Peoria, and finished with a dramatic climb up the fire escape to Shipper and Block's fifth-floor toy department. Hundreds of children reportedly waited there to give Santa their wish lists at his "Magical North Pole Workshop."

Photos taken with Macy's Santa enhanced the magical experience of meeting the big guy and also offered tangible evidence that, yes, there really is a Santa Claus.

Opposite: *In 1931 Marshall Field's Senior Designer Arthur Fraser created this Art Deco version of Santa's workshop for the window on the corner of State and Washington at the Chicago landmark.*

CAPTURED MOMENTS

Whether Santa arrived by foot, train, or fire escape, people embraced him wherever he went. Family outings to the local department store became an annual holiday ritual. In the 1930s, photography enhanced the experience. Now children could go home with a photograph of Claus as proof that he really did exist. The 1947 movie *Miracle on 34th Street* further confirmed the reality of Santa and set a new standard for department-store traditions.

For the next three decades, Santa took his place of honor on a royal throne at the end of a red carpet, and no matter how department stores embellished the scene, people came to anticipate the familiar thrill. Marshall Field's created the Cozy Cloud Cottage in 1948, which offered a snowy Santa village, mechanical elves, and gingerbread houses that diverted attentions while folks waited in line.

Macy's Santa's house, built in 1974, offered families a more private visit. "You would walk down a path with toy trains and then go into Santa's house," Rutan explains. The concept became so popular that Macy's had to enlarge the space just to accommodate the waiting line, which often grew to 900 people.

By 1977, Macy's Santa Land had a year-round dedicated space that occupied a significant part of the eighth floor, although it was open to the public only from the day after Thanksgiving through Christmas Eve. Santa Land expanded every year until 1979 when it drew 175,000 visitors. The number grew to 250,000 visitors by 1989, and it now exceeds 300,000 believers annually, coming from all 50 states and 104 countries around the world. When they're not at Macy's, they flock to other department stores to admire the lights and decorations, gaze in the windows, and sit for a few special moments with Santa.

Despite the Internet and mail-order catalogs, people still delight in going to department stores, not only to find gifts for others but for the gifts that Santa offers in return: promise, hope, and dreams that come true. ✦

Merry Mail

SANTA CLAUS SPRINKLES
HIS MAGIC THROUGH
THE MAIL AS HIS STAMPS HELP
DELIVER HOLIDAY WISHES
AROUND THE WORLD.

'Twas the Night before Christmas

U.S. POSTAGE 8c

Above: *Santa proudly toots his horn when he finally lands a place on an eight-cent U.S. postage stamp. Typographer and designer Bradbury Thompson created this premier 1972 Santa rendition.*

As Christmastime arrives with all its fanfare, our mailboxes burst with cards and letters. Bearing wishes from absent family members, faraway friends, and distant relations, the mail represents personal connections that for many happen just once a year. Seasonal greetings are a joy to anticipate and receive—not just for the warming thoughts inside but also for the special stamp on the envelope. What "present" will the Post Office deliver this year to help us herald the holiday season?

Written by Judith Stern Friedman ◆ *Photographs courtesy of the United States Postal Service*

Issued in 2001 and following the trend toward Victorian-era designs, these 34-cent turn-of-the-century Santas recall the days of simple celebration.

Six art directors work under contract to vary the look and style of each new release. The Postal Service issued this 20-cent traditional-Santa stamp in 1983.

SANTA SIGHTINGS

Besides Santa's regular appearance on stamps throughout the years, he's often found dropping in on these U.S. Post Offices whose names echo symbols of the Christmas season.

CITY AND STATE	ZIP CODE
Advent, WV	25231
Angeles, PR	00611
Angels Camp, CA	95222
Antler, ND	58711
Antlers, OK	74523
Blessing, TX	77419
Chestnut, IL	62518
Christmas, FL	32709
Faith, NC	28041
Faith, SD	57626
Frost, MN	56033
Frost, TX	76641
Holly, CO	81047
Holly, MI	48442
Joy, IL	61260
Mistletoe, KY	41351
Noel, MO	64854
North Pole, NY	12946
Partridge, KS	67566
Partridge, KY	40862
Rudolph, OH	43462
Rudolph, WI	54475
Santa, ID	83866
Santa Claus, IN	47579
Snow, OK	74567
Snowflake, AZ	85937
Starlight, PA	18461
Surprise, NY	12176
Wiseman, AR	72587

Other U.S. city names found in more than one state also are reminiscent of the holidays, including Bell, Bethlehem, Evergreen, Garland, Hope, and Nazareth.

The festive stamps that validate our mail add to Christmas lore and celebrations. Christmas cards were sent as early as the 1800s, but holiday postage stamps are a much more recent development. According to Terry McCaffrey, Manager of Stamp Development for the United States Postal Service, Christmas stamps first appeared in 1962, with the idea that they would complement holiday greeting cards.

It wasn't until 1972—a decade after the first Christmas issue—that Santa Claus made his stamp debut. In the three decades since, the Postal Service has issued only sixteen total Santa designs, although artists are constantly sketching new variations. "We try to space Santa throughout the program over the years," McCaffrey says.

SIZING UP

Originally measuring just ⅞ inch wide and 1 inch high, a postage stamp has inherent artistic limitations—its image must be reproduced clearly in a very small space. When the Postal Service realized greater efficiencies in the early 1990s, they were able to free up some space by increasing the size to 1 inch by 1⅛ inches.

"We found we could produce the stamps in large quantities and began printing them by the billions," McCaffrey explains. Today, a typical print run of Christmas stamps is 1.2 billion, matched in quantity only by the "Love" stamps. Other commemorative stamps, intended for collecting rather than mailing, are printed in quantities of 80 million to 150 million. The Elvis Presley commemorative stamp enjoyed a run of 500 million run, still less than half that of the revered Saint Nicholas stamps.

Collectors probably value Santa stamps more for sentimental reasons than for their monetary worth. Christmas stamps are issued in mid-October and stay on sale until the following September, when the Post Office recalls and shreds any unused designs. According to McCaffrey, "the stamps go up in value

Top: *Peter Good of Massachusetts designed this simple Santa stamp in 1994. "We were trying for a contemporary graphic approach as opposed to the realistic-looking Santa," explains Terry McCaffrey, U.S. Postal Service Manager of Stamp Development.*

Middle: *In 1984, the Postal Service requested designs done by children. The committee chose this drawing by 9-year-old Danny LaBiotta from several thousand submissions because it would reproduce well in a small area.*

Bottom: *"We're always trying to come up with something new," says McCaffrey. At the time, this 1979 Gingerbread Santa was "hot out of the oven."*

only if a smaller quantity is actually used." Most issues immediately double in value at the time they're retired, but they don't always continue to appreciate after that. The oldest 1972 Santa stamp, for instance, originally issued at 8 cents each, still is valued at only 20 cents. For insight on the value of other Santa stamps and commemorative issues, McCaffrey recommends the *U.S. Postal Service Guide to U.S. Stamps*, a softbound, full-color illustrated guide that can be found at bookstores and major post offices.

Another notable postage milestone was the self-adhesive stamp, also known as no-licks, pressure-sensitives, or "stickies." First introduced on a 1974 limited holiday dove-of-peace issue, self-adhesive stamps became widespread by the early 1990s. Now

Art director Dick Sheaff was inspired by his personal Victorian ephemera collection to create these classic Santa scenes. Theses 1995 issues stamps are two in a series of four; the other two show Victorian children at Christmas.

the public could send greeting cards en masse without ever having to lick a single stamp. Today, of the Postal Service's total stamp production, more than 90 percent are pressure-sensitives.

MAKING CHOICES

Deciding what goes on a U.S. postage stamp requires evaluating some 50,000 letters annually from citizens who write to suggest a spectrum of subjects. Beginning in 1957, a Citizens' Stamp Advisory Committee was formed to review all the commemorative possibilities, including people, endangered animals, historical events, and humanitarian causes.

Following specific Postal Service parameters, the fifteen appointed members meet quarterly to narrow down the choices. All U.S. stamps must feature American-related themes, and the subject matter must be national in scope. Commemorative anniversaries are considered only when the events occurred 50, 100, 150, or 200 years ago.

Once the Advisory Committee agrees on a slate of acceptable stamp designs, the Postal Service enlists artists to execute them. Six art directors oversee the process, contracting drawings from professionals and children or drawing from their own stock of photographs and other images. Christmas is so popular, McCaffrey says, that his office is often challenged to come up with ideas that haven't been done before.

Santa Claus, Saint Nick, and his many alter egos were natural inclusions for the Christmas-theme stamps. The first 1972 issue is noteworthy for its familiar Norman Rockwell style. Although Bradbury Thompson is the illustrator on record, his associate, Steven Dohanos (former member of the Advisory Committee), had illustrated for *The Saturday Evening Post* and probably influenced Thompson's work.

No matter how many variations of Santa stamps are issued, the man is sure to find his way to our hearts—not just down the chimney but also through the mail. ✦

1991 USA CHRISTMAS

1991 USA CHRISTMAS

1991 USA CHRISTMAS

1991 USA CHRISTMAS

1991 USA CHRISTMAS

Illustrated by John Berkey of Minnesota, this 1991 stamp booklet featured five different scenes depicting Santa's Christmas Eve journey.

The good behavior of these two delightful little girls has earned them a bounty of beautiful toys, including a child-size auto.

What could be more delightful than being surrounded by Santas? Today's Santa-lovers can find the object of their affections in a wide range of materials, from European vintage postcards to unique glass ornaments made from molds.

TIMELESS MEMORABILIA

Père Noël by Post

VINTAGE FRENCH HOLIDAY POSTCARDS ARE MORE
THAN SOUGHT-AFTER COLLECTIBLES.
IN A VERY REAL SENSE, THEY'RE ALSO PRECIOUS PICTORIAL
RECORDS OF THE COUNTRY'S HISTORY AND CUSTOMS.

Florence Theriault never set out to collect French postcards. The doll and toy expert who is the cofounder of Theriault's the Dollmasters, a leading appraisal and auction house, merely began seeking them out as a way to identify and date her dolls and toys. For years, she's traveled to France every few months to check out street markets, antiques dealers, auction houses, and the famous Paris flea markets to support her auction business. The former librarian, who's always had a passion for documenting her finds, started her postcard collection simply, "one by one by one." But every once in a while, she would locate a real find—an entire album of postcards saved from holiday seasons long ago.

So just what is the magnetic appeal of these artfully arranged and photographed little vignettes? Often painted in sepia tones or pastels, they were popular as greeting cards from about 1890 to 1920. But beyond simple greetings, they're also a visual panorama of Christmas customs during those nostalgic decades. The decorations on the trees, the clothing, the toys held by the children, even the demeanor of Father Christmas himself—they're all clues to how life was lived in France as the nineteenth century drew to a close.

Above: *A Père Noël brandishes a parcel of branches as a child admires a beautiful bisque doll,* left. *And a winsome pair of pajama-clad children woo Père Noël for some toys,* right.

Written by Allison Engel ✦ *Photographs courtesy of Gold Horse Publishing*

Heureux Noël

*A trio of children stands at the feet of this Père Noël. The rose-gowned angel appears
to be helping by offering up a woven basket containing a bisque-headed clown.*

A simply garbed St. Nicholas arrives in a flurry of snowflakes,
bearing a small tree, two homespun dolls, and a wrapped package.

KODAK MOMENTS

The photographs often were taken at commercial photography studios. Generally, children were posed with Santa in family settings, both indoors and out. Some were studio-arranged scenes with generic child models, but many were decorated vignettes that families could use as backdrops for their own relatively inexpensive personalized holiday cards.

The children and parents who were depicted tended to be from the middle and upper-middle classes and invariably were dressed in all their finery. Their costumes ranged from Little Lord Fauntleroy outfits and sailor suits for young boys to lavish lace dresses for little girls; it was nothing but formal attire for the fathers and velvet and lace gowns for the mothers. In the postcards that appeared around 1920, the costumes are a bit simpler and even reflect the flapper influence.

Among the most popular postcard designs were children and parents gathered around a decorated Christmas tree, photographs of costumed Santa Clauses, children holding Christmas gifts, and bundled-up children posed in front of snowy backdrops. Hearth scenes also were popular card motifs, and the mantels in the background might be embellished with candelabras, fresh flowers, small toys, or elaborately decorated urns or clocks. "These postcards send a message of what was popular at the time," Florence observes. "For example, as World War I drew close, you saw more toy rifles, more dolls in military costumes, and more nurse dolls."

CUSTOMS ON DISPLAY

The cards send another important message: They make clear the differences between French and other European Christmas customs. The wispy feather trees and spindly fir Christmas trees with their dangerously real candles so proudly on display would be considered throwaways by American standards, says Florence. "The French tend to underdecorate their trees." Many trees were designed for tabletops, and some weren't even trees at all.

The French Father Christmases were just as spindly as the trees. The old gent was portrayed as a tall, thin, bearded man dressed in a blue or beige robe who often as not carried twigs to give to "bad" boys and girls. *Aux méchants des verges!* ("To the naughty children, the branches!") is the message on a card showing a monklike St. Nicholas holding a handful of sticks. What a far cry from the fat, jolly fellow always laden with toys who's become our American counterpart.

Hand-tinted photographic postcards also were popular at Easter but oddly never were produced for

These two little girls seem to be offering Père Noël a fair trade—holly greens for one of the bisque dolls in his pack. Hand-lettered onto the card are the girls' names, Camille and Gilberte, and the date.

patriotic holidays, Mother's Day, or any other calendar event. The holiday cards disappeared after World War I, when the French doll industry was overtaken by German dollmakers.

CALLING ALL COLLECTORS

Of course, postcard collectors prize these holiday cards, but they're not alone. Enthusiasts who collect French dolls and toys also look for postcards that depict items in their collections. Fortunately for both camps, holiday postcards still are relatively affordable and can be bought for $5 to $25 each.

Most postcard collectors display their treasures in albums, but framing also is popular. Florence recommends dry-mounting postcards under nonglare glass using conservation-quality papers.

For fledgling collectors who visit France, Florence recommends seeking out the many street fairs. Almost

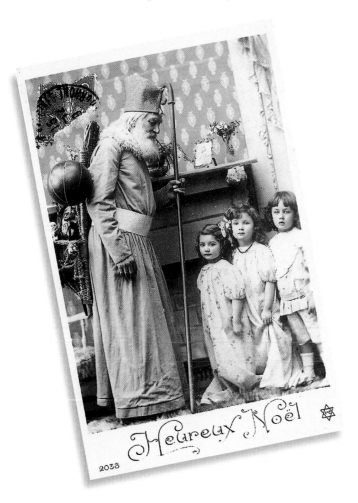

every week of the year, there are street markets in Paris where "bedroom dealers," part-time antiques dealers who work from their homes, sell what they've found cleaning out attics and cellars. A hotel concierge may be able to direct you to these sales. Or simply look for the banners that proclaim *déballage* ("junk") or *brocante* ("collectibles to junk"). Another good resource is the French magazine *Aladdin* that lists local flea markets. One of Paris's best, according to Florence, is the one held every Saturday and Sunday morning at the Gate at Vanves.

But enough about the photographs on the front. What do the backs of these postcards reveal? Surprisingly, Florence says she rarely comes across unusual messages on her finds. Once, however, she purchased a vintage photo album that was unintentionally revealing. The family in the photos obviously vacationed in Marseilles every summer. But the record of those carefree trips ended abruptly upon the outbreak of World War I, she says, "which I found very poignant."

Now Florence is doing her part to chronicle the past. She's already catalogued more than a million dolls and toys and has authored some forty-plus books about them. It's the history and sociology behind the items that interest her most. "If it were just about the objects themselves, I'd have lost interest," she says. "But themes repeat themselves as society changes, and you can see them recorded in the dolls and toys." More than a hundred postcards in her personal collection have been catalogued and reprinted in her book, *All I Want for Christmas: Antique Dolls and Toys in Vintage Photographs*, available from Gold Horse Publishing, Inc. For a charming glimpse at Christmases past and a preview of trends that may come again, holiday postcards are scraps of history worth preserving. ✦

These three little girls have had a peek inside Père Noël's sack of gifts filled with dolls, toys, and novelties galore.

Joyous children gather round this Père Noël bearing gifts—
including a beautiful bisque-head doll with flirty eyes.

It Takes Two

A CHRISTMAS TREE WITHOUT SANTA IS LIKE A SLEIGH WITHOUT REINDEER. TWO CINCINNATI TWIN SISTERS AGREED AND TOOK THE IDEA STRAIGHT TO THE BANK.

Above: *A small evergreen sprig of feathers was common on vintage Santas.*

Opposite: *Of the one hundred Santas handmade by the women, two of the most popular are the eight-inch Santa with a pack* left, *carrying a muslin bag filled with bottle-brush trees, pinecones, and berries, and the Santa candy container* right, *whose feet pull away to reveal a hidden compartment for candy and treats.*

More than twenty years ago, Sharen Bauer became smitten with a friend's dainty holiday feather tree. She told her identical twin sister, Karen, about her discovery, and soon Karen was on a mission to find her own trees. These tabletop treasures would certainly complement her growing collection of vintage Santas and ornaments, Karen reasoned.

The only problem: They just weren't to be found at local flea markets and antiques shows because so many other Christmas collectors were in the same pursuit. By this time, Karen also had accumulated plenty of ornaments that would be perfect for feather trees—so many that she even said to her sister, "If I could make these trees myself, I'd have them in every room."

Written by Debra Gibson ✦ *Photographs by Jeff Ricus*

WHAT'S A FEATHER TREE?

Feather trees might be considered the first artificial holiday trees. Typically, they are made from goose feathers that are cleaned and often hand-dyed. The feathers are woven or coiled around stiff wire to become the tree branches. These branches then are inserted into a wooden rod or dowel that serves as the tree trunk, which then is mounted on a wooden base. Many times, small berries are wired onto the ends of the branches to complete the tree.

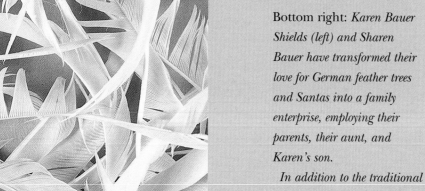

Bottom right: *Karen Bauer Shields (left) and Sharen Bauer have transformed their love for German feather trees and Santas into a family enterprise, employing their parents, their aunt, and Karen's son.*

In addition to the traditional holiday trees and patriotic trees, the sisters are beginning to market music-box trees, hanging wall trees, Victorian trees, and hall trees.

And with that came the creation of Twins Feather Trees in 1984, based in the women's hometown of Cincinnati, Ohio. Their first feather tree was a replica of a flea-market find, made from goose feathers and mounted on a wooden base created by the women's father. Though early sales at crafts shows were disappointing, a magazine article about the business that appeared in 1985 gave the company the recognition—and orders—it needed.

SO HAPPY TOGETHER

Feather trees—also called Nuremberg trees—originated in Germany in the mid-1800s as an alternative to freshly cut trees, which were becoming scarce. The original trees came in kits consisting of wires wrapped with feathers, a wooden trunk, and a painted base, which was either round or square. The kits even appeared in the Sears Roebuck catalog in the 1920s.

Soon after Sharen and Karen began selling their own feather trees, it became clear to them that something was missing—Santa. Their first St. Nick, similar to a German original, was a cotton-batting creation with the face, hands, and boots all made from antique molds. Sharen recalls another early Santa that met with an untimely end. "I'd taken apart an antique mini-Santa to make my molds. He was small and quite expensive," she recalls. "After he was molded, I put him back together. Unfortunately, my dog loved papier-mâché and plaster, and he completely demolished the Santa. All I have left are the clothes."

Determined to make authentic-looking Santas, Sharen asked an acquaintance in Colorado to teach her to make realistic face molds. Most of her face molds are made of plaster, which is set

A completed feather tree is mounted on a painted block of wood, much like one on the original versions.

into another mold. Only the boots and hands are made from rubber molds.

The bodies then are wired and wrapped to give them shape and bendable joints. "These aren't soft, plush toys," Sharen says. Instead, the Santas are configured as figurines and candy containers. The fabrics for the costumes, which often come from yard sales or flea markets, are stained or faded to give them an old-fashioned appearance. The artists create the

beards from wool or rabbit fur, and Sharen paints most of the faces.

To keep the Santas true to their German roots, the sisters make their expressions simple and stern, and they don't encumber them with lots of toys. Most of their Santas are based on originals from the early twentieth century.

THE WISH LIST

The shop's Santas range in price from $28 for the miniature Father Christmas in white batting to $185 for the larger patriotic Santas. If Sharen had to pick a favorite, it would be "the original white Father Christmas," she says. "He's just really pretty, and he's been with us since 1985. People still like him, and he still sells." The feather trees, which range in size from seventeen inches to eight feet, cost anywhere from $80 to $1,180. The sisters' father, a longtime cabinetmaker and woodworker, also makes the wicker, picket, and feather fences that are included as accessories.

The company, which employs eight full-time staffers, produces only about a hundred Santas each year. They're marketed at crafts shows, at the shop's annual Christmas open house, and on the company's Web site.

What keeps the sisters going after nearly twenty years of crafting Santas and feather trees? "We're making things we collect and like ourselves," Sharen says. "We have a true understanding of what they should look like, and we certainly have an appreciation for them." ✦

Replicated old-world Santas are a favorite with Twins Feather Trees customers. This candy container sports the traditional faded red coat with a string belt, a rabbit-fur beard, and a feather sprig.

Right: *Here's how he comes together. Cardboard cylinders serve as the core of the soft-sculpture bodies. A smaller cylinder is affixed to the boots. Once the Santa is completed, the two cylinders (which can be filled with candy) are inserted into one another.*

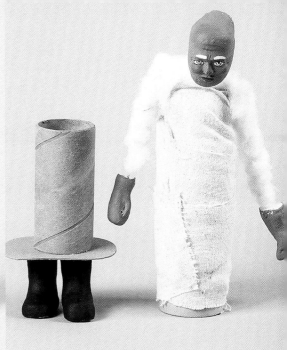

Above and Center: *This particular container, called* Santa on Snowball, *stands thirteen inches tall and sells for about $85.*

Left and Center: *These old-world pieces start with molded parts.*

A True Christmas Fairy Tale

THESE BLOWN-GLASS HEIRLOOMS NOT ONLY ARE A SIGHT
TO BEHOLD—THEY ALSO HAVE A DELIGHTFUL STORY TO TELL.

Above: *Fifteen-year-old apprentice Heinz Müller-Blech is taught by his uncle, a twelfth-generation glassblower, in this 1948 photo.*

Opposite: *Delicate wire trim and old-world Santa scraps grace these intricate glass works of art.*

Christmas-tree ornaments tell fascinating stories of family life and human experience, but few tell stories quite like the ornaments of inge-*glas*™, a company with a legacy that spans fourteen generations and four-hundred-plus years. Beginning with the advent of glassblowing tradition in Lauscha, Germany (just north of Bavaria), this is the fairy-tale adventure of a family that preserved its precious heritage through times of war, survival, and technological change.

Today, inge-*glas* ornaments are distributed worldwide, and many are produced from original antique molds that date back to the 1850s. These blown-glass treasures are known for their exquisite expressions,

Written by Judith Stern Friedman ✦ Photographs by Marty Baldwin

painted details, and translucent sheen. A stern-faced Santa warns, "You'd better be nice," while a jolly elf in glasses checks his list twice. Angels, snowmen, reindeer, and bells all are rendered in brilliant three-dimensional shapes that bring merriment and meaning to Christmas trees the world over.

THE BREATH OF BEAUTY

Fashioning inge-*glas* ornaments demands skills that have been honed for generations. Starting with just a flame and a six-foot-long glass tube, the German artisans soften the glass and roll it between their hands. Then they gently blow it into the shape of a free-form ball and place it into a two-piece ceramic mold, which resembles the halves of a walnut shell (the metal and slate molds used by other companies don't produce such fine detail). After blowing one more time to set the shape, the artisans pop the glass out of the molds. Although the glass may take only seconds to mold, the finishing process can take up to a week.

Silvering is the next step, in which the inside of the ornament is coated with a silver-nitrate layer that creates an opaque sheen. After the piece is dipped in a fast-drying lacquer, the details are hand-painted on, one color at a time. Only then is the ornament glittered, signed, and numbered. Finally, the company's signature Star Crown, a metal suspension ring in the shape of a five-pointed star, is placed on top as the finishing touch.

A LONG-LIVED LEGACY

Perhaps most remarkable is the fact that this business has survived and remained in the same family for more than four centuries. In 1596, in the Bavarian forests of

The jolly ol' elves in this sled are making merry while holding armfuls of trees and gifts.

Lauscha, Germany, Christoff Müller built *das Hultenplatz*, or "the foundry place." It was here that he designed everything from blown-glass vessels, vases, and perfume bottles to children's marbles and Christmas ornaments—all reflecting the current-day influences of church and aristocracy.

Generations of Müllers continued to master the art of glassblowing, and by the ninth generation, the suffix "Blech" was added to the family name. This German word for "metal" was a nod to the trademark suspension ring that characterized their ornaments.

A turning point came in 1846, when Queen Victoria and Prince Albert (he came from Germany originally) popularized the notion of hanging German glass ornaments on the Christmas tree. People the world over were fascinated with this high-profile couple and imitated their every move—even as far away as America. By the 1850s, the Müller-Blechs had seized the opportunity to export their blown-glass goods to the United States through a distribution arrangement with Woolworth's in Pennsylvania. Over the next decade, imported German Christmas-tree ornaments would become an American status symbol.

PACKING IT UP

Until 1947, the Müller-Blech family thrived in Lauscha, but post-World War I Russia eventually threatened their freedom there. Fourteen-year-old Heinz Müller-Blech was determined to escape Communist influence. His father had been killed in World War I by a Russian sniper, and Heinz had been sustaining his family by trading their blown-glass ornaments with American

A simple feather tree is the traditional German way to display Christmas ornaments.

Opposite: *At last, the final ornament is placed upon the tree. Glass tree toppers crown the trees of homes the world over.*

soldiers and their wives in exchange for essential food and provisions.

In 1953, in the last days of the "Green Wall" (before Lauscha would become heavily patrolled and mined), Heinz gathered up his father's tools and escaped from western Germany to Bavaria's northernmost point, Neustadt by Coburg, a small town of only a few thousand people. Through the mail and with the help of American GIs, Heinz managed to rescue many of

the antique molds he'd left behind. Friends and relatives who had recovered them from destroyed Lauschian buildings sent them to him covertly for safekeeping, sometimes in pieces.

In Neustadt, Heinz continued the family tradition, setting up shop and starting a family of his own (the current company name was chosen to honor his wife, Inge). While Heinz's son, Klaus, was becoming the fourteenth-generation Müller-Blech to enter the business, another glassblowing family was indoctrinating its daughter, Birgit Eichhorn Jeremias-Sohn. In true storybook fashion, in 1992 the young artisans met at an ornament-collector's convention in Reading, Pennsylvania, and fell in love.

A MATCH MADE IN NEUSTADT

The marriage of these two young people also was a marriage of two glassblowing legacies. The result was inge-*glas* workshops, a three-hundred-thousand-square-foot factory, still in Neustadt, that houses a collection of six thousand antique glassblowing molds, thousands of newly created molds, and a team of one hundred highly skilled workers who themselves come from a long line of European artisans. A separate mold department preserves the ornaments' integrity by refurbishing or reproducing antique molds and building new ones on commission. Although European distribution represents the bulk of the company's business, in 2000 inge-*glas* redirected its American

Ceramic molds are used to capture the intricate detail of each ornament.

Opposite: *The most filigreed treasures originated from the glass workshops of old and were created with great detail and technical skill. The unique combination of molded and free-blown glass is testament to the glassblower's expertise and the endless hours of practice needed to create these masterpieces.*

distribution to its own facility in Ashland, Virginia, under the name Inge's Christmas Heirlooms.

Working year-round, inge-*glas* produces millions of items each year, ranging in size from one inch to two feet tall and including ornaments, tree toppers, and mantel pieces—all of which sell for $3 to $110 each. Of the twelve hundred ornament styles issued annually, 2002's top sellers included the Bride's Tree, a grouping of twelve wishes for newlyweds; Baby's First Christmas, a six-piece set; and the new Holy Night Scene of twelve boxed Christmas ornaments.

As the fifteenth generation of Müller-Blechs comes of age, they're likely being groomed for the inge-*glas* family business. And as their story continues to be written, others can attach their own families' stories to the ornaments that are part of this true Christmas fairy tale. ✦

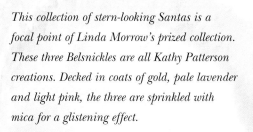

This collection of stern-looking Santas is a focal point of Linda Morrow's prized collection. These three Belsnickles are all Kathy Patterson creations. Decked in coats of gold, pale lavender and light pink, the three are sprinkled with mica for a glistening effect.

Christmas is close to these collectors' hearts...and close at hand. It's also embodied in the Santa treasures they proudly display at Christmastime and often year-round.

DEVOTED COLLECTORS

Old Friends

THIS SANTA COLLECTOR DISCOVERED AN UNEXPECTED
SURPRISE IN HER PURSUIT OF KRIS KRINGLE—
FELLOW FANATICS WHO'VE BECOME FAST FRIENDS.

*This turn-of-the century Santa,
also a candy container, features an
antique feather sprig, a wicker
basket, and a paper lantern.*

Opposite: *This Santa is artist
Kathy Patterson's very first,
a thirty-four-inch papier-mâché
candy container with a wool
felt coat. It's posed alongside an
antique sheep pull toy.*

L
inda Morrow found true love at the Pasadena
Rose Bowl. It was at a swap meet there that she
purchased her very first Santa. Made of cardboard
and perched atop a cardboard sleigh pulled by white
celluloid reindeer (made in Japan), he cost little. But
that unassuming doll launched a nearly twenty-year
love affair with St. Nick.

Today, the California nurse-practitioner owns close
to a hundred Santas, both antique and contemporary.
Although most of them are displayed only during
the holidays, she readily admits that her Christmas
celebrations extend "well into the New Year."

Though Christmas has been her "absolute favorite
holiday" since childhood, Linda didn't begin acquiring
Santas until she read about vintage collections in

Written by Debra Gibson ✦ *Photographs by Ed Gohlich*

magazines. She counts Connecticut collector Bob Merck as a major influence. "Every Santa article and book I read seemed to mention his collections," Linda says. "He's been so generous over the years in sharing his inspiration. I'd look at his pieces and say, 'Oh my gosh, I want something like that.'"

Above: *Some of Linda's favorites include (from left): a Kathy Patterson Belsnickle complete with hand-blown glass icicles for a beard; a vintage Santa from the late 1800s clothed in a silvery metallic gauze coat; a Roberta Taylor "nodder" with a chimney-topped roof on his head; and another Kathy Patterson twenty-four-inch Santa in a hat decorated with antique waxlike fruits and holding an assortment of antique metal miniatures.*

Opposite: *Linda's collection features vintage pieces like the two in the foreground, both made in Germany between 1890 and the early 1900s, as well as more contemporary works created by artists Kathy Patterson and Roberta Taylor.*

THE THRILL OF THE HUNT

After her initial purchase at the Rose Bowl, Linda and a cousin discovered the delights of scavenging for small red Japanese pipe-cleaner Santas with reddish clay faces. "We'd find them for $2 to $9 each and think we'd really scored," she recalls. That hunt eventually led to a yen for the slightly larger Japanese cotton-batting Santa figures.

When Linda began researching the history of Santa collecting, she quickly gravitated toward antique German pieces. Most of her finds came from antiques shows, but she also had good luck at flea markets and at the Glendale All-American Toy and Advertising Show.

She considers her first "important" Santa to be one she bought in the late 1980s. He was made in Germany between 1910 and 1920 and has "a wonderful face and beard," Linda says. "He's one of my favorites because he was my first 'major' Santa and he has such a great expression." And he also has an index finger pointing toward the ground, a fragile component that has survived for nearly a hundred years.

Another vintage Santa that ranks high on Linda's list of favorites is a "not very showy" figurine who carries a linen bag on his back. The small papier-mâché head of a little boy peeks out from the top of the bag, and bellows on the figurine make the little boy cry. "He must be one of those Santas who picked up all the bad little children and carried them off," Linda explains.

Other antique favorites include a Santa driving a Lufa sleigh while wearing a pink coat dusted with gold glitter as well as a small Santa riding sidesaddle on a white donkey, complete with tiny stirrups dangling below his feet.

ENTHUSIASTS UNITE

Linda attributes her impressive vintage collection to her membership in Golden Glow, a nonprofit organization that unites Christmas collectors from across the nation. "My favorite thing is to go to convention every July," she says. "I've met some wonderful friends there and bought some amazing Santas. We all share a love of Christmas. Once I went, I was hooked."

It was through one of those friends that Linda met a New York City actor who often traveled to California for auditions. He also was a Santa collector and dealer, and under his tutelage, she substantially added to her collection of vintage Santas. "It was magical," Linda says. "I got to shop at my dining room table. Not only did he have many Santas but a fabulous Dresden

Linda shows off her antique holly boxes while standing in front of a collection of antique cotton-batting ornaments.

Opposite: *A collection of Belsnickles makes quite a statement standing at attention on top of an antique cupboard.*

collection as well. He'd open these boxes, and I'd just gasp. I got such wonderful things from him."

Of the nearly three dozen antique Santas Linda owns, candy containers predominate. But her collection also includes a Santa lantern, postcards, and chocolate molds, and she has late-1800s Santa antique blocks by the McLaughlin Company made of vibrantly colored litho paper over wood. There's also a red wooden Santa wagon, complete with a blue plaque on its side inscribed, "St. Claus, Dealer in Good Things."

In addition, Linda owns Santa advertising plates dating back to the early 1900s, as well as many antique paper trading cards, pictures, images, and books. Once she even found a cloth stocking cut from old Santa fabric wadded in the bottom of a basket of old letters and family photos that she'd received from an uncle in Minnesota. "I was so thrilled," she says of the discovery.

But Linda admits that great vintage finds are getting tougher to track down. "Antique Santas are getting

scarcer and so much more expensive," she says. "Yet, when you're hooked, however you can work it out, you do. eBay has certainly made a dent in things—more people are aware of what's out there. I don't like to buy online because I want to look at my Santas—and touch them and smell them—before I buy. I have to fall in love with a Santa before I'll take it."

FRESH FACES

Some of her more recent "crushes" have come courtesy of contemporary Santa artists. In particular, Debbee Thibault, Roberta Taylor, and Kathy Patterson have found a loyal patron in Linda, who displays their works—fifty to sixty newer Santas—throughout her home year-round. "I think they're three of the most talented new artists making traditional Santas," Linda says, "They're just doing phenomenal work, and they've all become good friends," she adds.

But there's always room for another vintage Santa. Linda recently acquired a Santa candy container with a note rolled up and tucked into the bottom. The note, dated December 1912 at St. Joseph, Missouri, reads in part: "To our Patsy: We wish you much joy and happiness this Christmas. May it be the best you ever have and the worst you ever have."

That same joy and happiness also are evident when Linda decorates her home with her many Santas, including six trees in her bedroom alone. "From the

An antique Santa candy container revealed an extraspecial sentiment, a handwritten note dated December 1912.

Opposite: Among Linda's most prized possessions are about fifty vintage Santa postcards dating from the late 1800s to around 1915.

first time I saw collectible Santas, I felt an instant connection," she explains. "I couldn't believe things like this actually existed."

But even more special than the Santas she accumulates are the friends Linda has collected over the years who love the holidays as much as she does. "I've met so many fabulous people in my years as a Santa collector," she says. "I probably wouldn't have met any of them otherwise. I treasure each one, and their friendships will always be more important to me than how many Santas I own." ✦

A Few of Her Favorite Things

CHANCE ENCOUNTERS LEAD TO EXQUISITE ACQUISITIONS FOR THIS COMMITTED SANTA COLLECTOR.

Above: *This thirty-two-inch soft-sculpture Santa stands out in Dana's collection due to its beautifully molded face, glass eyes, and vintage feather tree and bells.*

Opposite: *Wisconsin wood-carver Tony Costanza created this eighteen-inch tabletop figurine especially for Dana, knowing her love of rabbits. The Santa atop its back is removable.*

For Dana Miller Wade, the equation is simple: Like the artist, love the Santas.

This California collector has amassed a stunning array of Santas over the past decade—about three hundred at last count. But while other enthusiasts may base their purchases on a particular medium or costume, Dana likes to get to know the artists before ever pursuing their creations. Consequently, today she owns spectacular one-of-a-kind Santas from artists nationwide—a collection that got its start with a chance introduction to a now-famous holiday artist.

"One night, I went to a tiny local shop that was sponsoring a guest appearance by Christopher Radko," Dana recalls. "I picked up one of his ornaments —this was before he was so well known—and then I got to

Written by Debra Gibson ✦ *Photographs by Ed Gohlich*

meet him. He was so delightful and charming that I had to turn around, go back into the store, and buy about twenty more of his ornaments. That's what started me on Christmas."

At about this same time, Dana learned of the Santas that were being produced by Massachusetts artist Judi Vaillancourt. When Judi's husband, Gary, made an appearance near Dana's home, the two met. "I was charmed by their company's story and history," Dana says, and soon she was among their most avid fans.

Those figurines are made from chalkware formed in antique chocolate molds and then intricately painted to resemble old-world Santas. Dana has become so smitten with Judi's work that she now travels to her Sutton, Massachusetts, studio each May for the annual collector's weekend. There, she's able to buy one-of-a-kind Santas along with the original molds from which they were made.

These Santas range in size from two inches to three feet tall. Some are Belsnickles, the stern Santa assistants of the 1800s who supposedly questioned little children about whether they'd been naughty or nice.

TIMELESS TREASURES

Paul Gordon is another of Dana's favorite Santa artists. She met him at a folk-art show in Wilton, Connecticut, "and I absolutely fell in love with his work," she says. Most of her six Gordon pieces stand two to four feet tall, but she has one that's life-size. That Santa remains on display year-round.

"That one is probably my favorite piece," Dana explains, "because he's just so beautiful you want to hug him. At Christmas, I fill his arms with feather trees, garlands, and toys, but he also holds flags for the Fourth of July and baskets at Easter."

Gordon's Santas are unique in that most of the heads are made from hollowed and painted gourds. "I fell in love with them because they're so whimsical," Dana says, adding that she also admires the antique fabrics and accessories that dress Gordon's pieces.

Fellow Californian Debbee Thibault is another of Dana's "artist finds," and the two women have become fast friends. Dana is proud to own some of Debbee's earliest originals, which were meticulously constructed by hand from fabric, cotton, and wire. These days, Debbee simply molds the pieces and fills them with a paper composition before painting them. To date, Dana owns about fifty of Debbee's Santas, ranging in size from three to twelve inches.

Above: *Artist Debbee Thibault designed the three current limited-edition Santas in the background, all molded and filled with a paper composition. One of her earlier pieces is shown riding a sled.*

Left: *In addition to Vaillancourt, Gordon, and other artists in her collection, Dana has a large assortment of Debbee Thibault's original pieces.*

And recently, Dana began collecting the Santas of Wisconsin wood-carver Tony Costanza, whose unique pieces now number about six in her collection. Vicki Smyers and Connie Krizner, who create old-world reproductions, also are well represented. "They're like antiques without the antique prices," Dana says of Vicki's and Connie's Santas.

THAT'S WHAT FRIENDS ARE FOR

Dana also has begun collecting the works of Roberta Taylor and Kathy Patterson, artists she discovered through friendships with other Santa devotees. "When I see the wonderful Santas in my friends' collections, I feel like I just have to have them for my own," Dana says. "I never intended to become this big of a collector—it just kind of happened. When you're out there shopping with other Christmas fanatics, it's easy to get caught up in the frenzy.

This one-of-a-kind chalkware Santa was hand-painted by Massachusetts artist Judi Vaillancourt from an antique German chocolate mold. Standing just over six inches tall, this Santa boasts exquisite detail, including individual brush-strokes on the coat.

Above: Dana shows off one of her favorite pieces, a life-size soft-sculpture Santa from artist Paul Gordon.

"But my friends and I know our boundaries," she says with a laugh. "If we happen to like the same piece, one of us always defers to the one who already collects that artist. And sometimes we even sell pieces to each other. I've probably met my best friends through collecting. It's so much fun to know people who enjoy the same things."

Out of loyalty to the artists she now patronizes, Dana isn't an across-the-board collector. "I don't like to buy everything that's out there," she explains. "Even if I like a certain piece, I won't buy it if it doesn't fit with the pieces in my collection."

Dana pursues new pieces year-round, especially on the East Coast. "Out here in California, there's just not too much Christmas to be found until fall," she says. "But when I go back East, I can find Christmas any time of the year."

And although she admits to being open to new artists, Dana says her ultimate collecting goal is just to stop. "I've run out of room! Either I stop, or I get another house. This all really happened by accident," she continues. "I didn't set out to start collecting Santas, but that sure happened pretty quickly. I just loved all the Santas these artists made, so I filled my home with them. They make me smile." ✦

More Debbee Thibault Santas are shown here, all standing about twenty inches tall. Even some accessories (toys, stuffed animals, and dolls) are handmade from paper. The Santa on the left with the red coat is one of the last originals made by Debbee herself in 1997.

Spirit of Christmas Past

PASSIONATE SANTA COLLECTORS STEVE AND DOTTIE WILT
HAVE AMASSED A TREASURE TROVE OF MUSEUM-QUALITY ANTIQUES.

Above: *Steve and Dottie Wilt share
an enthusiasm for collecting the antique
Christmas items that fill their home
during the holidays.*

Opposite: *Displaying their collections as
attractively as possible is part of the fun.
Here, vintage Christmas boxes, cards, fans,
and even matchbooks nestle in greenery
dotted with lights.*

His voice growing more excited with every word, Steve Wilt explains how he and his wife, Dottie, made the leap from casual Santa enthusiasts to avid collectors. "We didn't get started until 1988. We'd always admired a friend's wonderful assortment of Christmas items. One day we spotted an antique Santa for $15, so we snapped it up. That started the whole thing." The couple searches for pieces wherever they go, but auctions and estate sales are their favorite haunts. "Occasionally, we'll find something on an Internet site," Steve says, "but I like to see an item up close, turn it upside down, and touch it before I buy."

A COLLECTOR'S PARADISE

Living in York, Pennsylvania, in the heart of Lancaster County, Steve and Dottie credit their historic location for helping them grow their collection. "So many

Written by Shelley Stewart ✦ *Photographs by Randy Foulds*

American Christmas traditions began right here," Steve says. "The ninety-mile radius around York includes most of the area originally settled by German immigrants in the early 1700s." The settlers brought their customs with them, perhaps as a sentimental link to the country they'd left behind.

"This area is great for collectors," Steve says, "because so many residents are descendants of those immigrants." Christmas items from the old country often were passed from generation to generation. "We bought about a dozen paper ornaments from an elderly German lady," Steve says. "She remembered her grandmother decorating with them, and she even pointed out a couple of places where candles on the tree had singed the paper during her childhood."

Each passing year conspires to make less out of more, as delicate glass ornaments break, paper scraps tear, and plaster figures deteriorate. Even in this history-rich part of the country, early ornaments, figures, and toys are becoming hard to find. Items made as late as the 1930s are still fairly plentiful, though. "The heyday of imported decorations was in the latter part of the nineteenth century and the early part of the twentieth century," Steve says.

SPECTACULAR SCENERY

In the walk-out basement of their ranch-style home, they've devoted three walls to an incredibly detailed putz, or Christmas scene. "The word 'putz' means 'to decorate' in German," Steve says, "and I guess you could say that we really did it! First we built plywood tiers along the walls. Then I spray-painted heavy paper with various colors, crumpled the paper to

Over the years, a staggering variety of products have featured holiday images on the packaging. Vintage paper boxes often don't hold up very well, so those in good condition are much in demand.

Below left: *Colorful Santa pins were a popular form of advertising for stores in the early twentieth century.*

Assorted German Santas and Belsnickles look right at home in a setting of vintage brush trees and artificial snow. Gently glowing lights beneath the snow highlight the collection.

Stockings with intricately detailed chimneys, trees, and Santas are early examples of screen-printing.

Below: *Santa gets a nudge from soldiers on this World War II-era gift box.*

form uneven ridges, and attached it to the tiers with hot glue." Those paper "rocks" are the base for hundreds of tiny antique trees, buildings, people, and animals—all artfully arranged into an imaginative landscape.

Steve points out that almost all of the figures dotting that landscape came from the Erzgebirge region of Germany, formerly a mining district whose residents have a centuries-old tradition of carving. When the mines ceased to be productive, hungry miners turned to selling their detailed carvings. Whole families often specialized in a particular subject; some carved only animals, others only wagons. "Erzgebirge is a region

where all sorts of holiday novelties, including nodders and smokers, are still being made," Steve says.

"The putz is the only part of our collection that we leave on display all year," he points out. "When we designed the tiers, we planned it so the boxes holding the rest of our collection could be stored underneath and out of sight until the next year. We often forget what we have, so it's always fun when we open the boxes again."

Each year, they vary the way they decorate, but they always include a number of "themed" trees. "My favorite is the Patriotic Tree," Steve says. Although the tree is the essence of Americana, most of the ornaments were nevertheless made in Germany.

ORNAMENTS GALORE

After World War II, most of the skilled glassblowers ended up in East Germany, and their work was no longer available in the United States. "We went from handmade ornaments to mass-produced items almost overnight, and the quality suffered as a result. But now the quality has come back and the decorations are as good as ever," Steve says. "Dottie and I wrapped a bare-wire tree with cotton to resemble an antique tree. Then we decorated it with seven hundred brand-new blown-glass ornaments. It was absolutely beautiful!" He laughs as he predicts, "Yes, in about a hundred years, some other collector will be so excited about the ornaments of today." He should know: Times and taste may change, but collectors stay the same. ✦

MASTER CRAFTERS

The spirit of Christmas is
carried on from year to year in
the skillful hands—and generous
souls—of these master crafters.
Their inspired handiwork spreads
the wonders of Santa's loving
message to all whose
lives they touch.

*Wood takes shape in the hands of Vaughn
Rawson and is transformed into magical
works of art: our favorite gift givers.*

Photograph by Perry Struse

Carving Out His Niche

VAUGHN RAWSON LEARNED THE ANCIENT ART OF WOOD CARVING
FROM THE PRINTED PAGE. NOW HE'S WRITTEN A NEW CHAPTER FOR
SANTA COLLECTORS EVERYWHERE WITH HIS MINIMASTERPIECES.

Vaughn Rawson's destiny seemed all but preordained: His great-great-grandfather was a master carpenter and carver. "I own a pipe he whittled at Lookout Mountain while he was in Sherman's army during the Civil War," he proudly recounts. "I've also seen a church he built, and it's beautiful. I loved listening to stories about him, although I seem to be the only descendant who's inherited his knack for woodworking."

Indeed, Vaughn and his wife Stephanie designed and made their own furniture for the cozy home they built on seven wooded acres just outside Mason, Michigan. Furniture design was a joint effort, with Vaughn handling the construction and Stephanie the finishing. When they ran out of room for one more stick of furniture, they needed another creative outlet.

That's when Vaughn began to read books on wood carving to teach himself the venerable craft. "It took me forever, but I really enjoyed the learning process," he says. "Carving is an age-old art that's very low-tech. It's fascinating that almost every ancient culture has carving in its history, whether it's for religious pieces, animals, or other symbols. The antiquity of the art and the time it takes to produce a carving appealed to me."

Above: *Vaughn and Stephanie are happily surrounded by the tools of their trade.*

Opposite: *The Rawsons keep Vaughn's first example of each carving on display as a prototype. "They give us inspiration for new and different designs, and they keep us on track with our current designs," says Stephanie.*

Written by Kathy Roth Eastman ✦ *Photographs by Perry Struse*

FROM HOBBY TO CAREER

In time, carving gave the couple so much pleasure that in January 1992, both Vaughn and Stephanie quit full-time jobs and embarked on new careers as folk artists under the company name The Whimsical Whittler. Vaughn carved figures from basswood, and Stephanie painted them. At first, their style resulted in a smorgasbord of carvings. However, as customers requested more and more Christmas items, the artists began to specialize in Santas.

"We love Christmas," Vaughn is quick to add. "In fact, years ago I saw a carved Santa that I really admired; that got me interested in Santas. We're also fascinated with Thomas Nast, the illustrator who provided Civil War political cartoons to the *New York Illustrated News* that portrayed Santa visiting the troops. President Grant once said that no one did more to preserve the Union than Thomas Nast." Yet another reason to focus on Santas: "It's wonderful designing and carving a figure everyone knows, loves, and believes in, even though no one has ever really seen him. It leaves the design possibilities wide open."

The Rawsons' style developed quickly as they solidified their client base. "It took six or seven months to develop 'the Rawson style,' but once Vaughn went beyond the books he'd learned from, his imagination took over. That's when the fun began," Stephanie recalls. "Now it's very satisfying whenever someone tells us they can identify a piece as ours."

NEW-WORLD CRAFTSMANSHIP

It's the detailed carving that's the big giveaway. Some pieces have as many as fifteen tiny carved toys spilling out of Santa's bag. Others are jointed, capturing him bending over or looking over his shoulder.

The Whimsical Whittler updates its offerings each January, when Vaughn and Stephanie release brochures with the year's new designs. At any one time, they may offer forty to sixty designs, which they often

Here are three of the Rawsons' whimsical designs: Dream Maker (left), Celestial Ride (center), and Wheelbarrow Santa (right).

Opposite: *Shelves display the Rawsons' largest and most detailed Santas. These figures are up to seventeen inches tall and may contain as many as twenty carved toys. Most are interpretations of antique Santas inspired by Thomas Nast cartoons, postcards, and Santas from other countries.*

customize for their customers. One such favorite includes tiny reindeer on a rooftop that can be customized to look like the buyer's home.

The majority of the Whimsical Whittler line has an antique look, thanks to Stephanie's characteristic muted colors. But the line also includes whimsical characters that "make people smile," as Vaughn says. Many of these characters are inspired by antique Christmas cards, books, and toys, not to mention day-to-day living. For example, inspiration for one piece came from a nursery-rhyme poster the Rawsons saw at

The Eight Tiny Reindeer figure is, as Stephanie says, very magical. "People always ask, 'How do you do that?' because it looks like the sleigh is taking off and flying away." This figure is custom-designed using a model of the customer's home and toys that fit each household's unique personality.

a café. Visions of the sandman prompted Vaughn to carve Dream Maker, a Santa shown flying over the moon. Other carvings commemorate patriotism, world peace, and characters from literature, such as favorites from the novels of Charles Dickens.

Although he's the focal point of each carving, Santa may not be the first character to take shape. For example, in the Tin Man carving, the idea began with the jointed tin man. Only as the carving progressed did Vaughn decide what the accompanying Santa should look like.

According to the couple, the possibilities for future carvings are endless: "We have enough ideas for the next ten years of designs," they claim.

CREATING HAPPY CUSTOMERS

Part of the fun is interacting with customers old and new. "Our Nursery Rhyme Santa includes carvings of ten nursery-rhyme characters," Stephanie says. "We enjoy challenging people to correctly identify all of them. Only one person—she was from England, where the rhymes originated—has identified them all. There's a rhyme that has stumped everyone else."

One of the pleasures of working with such a light-hearted subject is witnessing the joy on buyers' faces. "It's very gratifying when a customer asks us to sign a figure for a grandchild, even though the grandparent may plan to display the figure for many Christmases to come," Stephanie says. "It will be passed on when the child is old enough to appreciate it. We know we play a role in many families' holiday traditions."

"Our carvings have put us in contact with some really nice people," Vaughn adds. "I guess you can't be an unpleasant person if you collect Santas." The Rawsons have many tales to tell of their wonderful customers. There's the group of West Coast women who order for each other every year and delight in discovering which Santa they'll find under the tree. There's the woman who has collected some forty Whimsical Whittler treasures and who considers

them to be as close as her own family. Then there are the children, who with tongues sticking out in concentrated effort, carve gifts for their mothers in the Rawsons' studio. "Of course, the mothers always cry when they get them," Stephanie says. In fact, even adults are so touched when they get a Whimsical Whittler carving for Christmas that it's not unusual for the Rawsons to receive thank-you phone calls—even on Christmas Day.

And now in the days, weeks, and months before the next holiday season, the Rawsons spend long hours producing their lovingly handcrafted pieces. "There's nothing better than watching the snow drift gently into the trees," Stephanie muses. "We're doing something we love in a place we love." ✦

Figgy Pudding, new for 2003, already is a favorite. "It just looks like he's striding out to deliver the pudding," Stephanie says. "We had an English customer who really warmed up to this Santa, because, of course, figgy pudding is a very British tradition."

Simply Vintage

NICOL SAYRE EXPRESSES HER PASSION FOR THE PAST IN HANDMADE SANTA DOLLS THAT TRANSCEND TIME.

At age forty, Nicol Sayre still plays with toys. She searches out candy canes and wool baby blankets—not for herself but for her Santa dolls. With every thumbprint on a sculpted face, every stitch in a jolly suit, and every treasure tucked under Santa's arms, Nicol recaptures the innocence of Christmas past.

Skillfully sculpted from papier-mâché and cloth, her merry men are a masterful mix of handmade garb, vintage trims, and vivid textures. From five-inch-tall fellows perched on vintage candy boxes to life-size figures riding sleighs, Nicol delivers joy in many sizes.

SUITING UP

"I like my Santas to look like they've been around for a hundred years," Nicol says. Although the facial expressions are simple—just painted eyes and rosy cheeks—Nicol's art has taken more than thirteen years to evolve.

Since taking up her craft—which is solely self-taught—Nicol has experimented with cloth, polymer clay, and now papier-mâché, which she says results in a more old-fashioned look. Using a mix she concocted after much trial and error, she sculpts the face, nose, cheeks, eyebrows, and sometimes the boots, depending on the doll. Then she leaves the pieces to dry, often for several days.

"The faces seem to make themselves," Nicol says, stressing that she doesn't use a mold. "Each one turns out completely different." Using acrylic paints, she highlights the features, focusing on the warm and friendly eyes. Once she's satisfied with the expression,

Written by Judith Stern Friedman ✦ *Photographs by Jamie Hadley*

This one-of-a-kind Santa expresses a simple sentiment and sets the mood for celebration.

Opposite: *Nicol Sayre's style has evolved over thirteen years of crafting Santas. Her most recent figures tend to have lighter, whiter, more wintry colors.*

Many Santas stand on boxes reminiscent of early candy containers. The boxes are decorated with copies of pen-and-ink flourishes and lined with Christmas papers.

Good Children

collections: timeworn fabrics, old cotton batting, chenille candy canes, beaded garlands, toys, and trinkets.

When Nicol can't find vintage objects, she calls on her collection of antique Christmas books, postcards, and collectible papers to make her own reproductions. She might copy pages from an 1860 book and use them to shape cornucopias for her Santas to hold. "I also have several handwritten letters from the 1830s that I copy and use to line my candy boxes," Nicol says. Sometimes she looks for books that are falling apart and incorporates the actual pages in her work. "You just can't reproduce the feel of old paper," she says.

she applies a crackle glaze and another coat of antiquing medium to create an aged effect.

For the body, she wraps cotton batting around a wire armature and then sews the clothes to fit the form. The head is attached with a wooden dowel or wire, and the wool mohair beard is affixed with tacky glue. "Sometimes I sketch out ideas," Nicol says. Other times, flea-market finds inspire her. A vintage display case might prescribe Santa's size, or an old embroidered quilt may suggest his suit. French linen sheets make perfect pants, and a child's fur cape is ideal to cut up for trim. "There's a lot of hand-stitching," Nicol says, which accounts for much of her treasures' vintage appeal.

STUFFING THE SACK

Monthly trips to flea markets and antiques stores help Nicol build her stockpile of Santa supplies. "I use a lot of antique tinsel and old ornaments," she says. Her studio in Pleasanton, California (about forty miles east of San Francisco), is a haphazard array of cubbyhole

Above: *The smaller Santas range in size from five inches to fourteen inches and recall traditional Christmas scenes.*

Right: *A lucky find of old-brick-patterned paper inspired this Santa. He holds a paper cornucopia, a handmade glitter star, and an old-fashioned brush tree.*

GROUNDED IN TRADITION

Besides drawing inspiration from her antiques collections, Nicol instinctively connects to the past and to her family's German heritage. "I was fascinated by historical costumes and always wished I could wear a hoop skirt," she says. Born and raised in California, she now lives only two miles from the home where she grew up. She learned to sew at age eight from her dressmaker mother, and her favorite girlhood book was *Little House on the Prairie* by Laura Ingalls Wilder, which epitomizes the simplicity Nicol so appreciates.

Though hoop skirts never came back into style, Nicol studied fashion merchandising at a local college and then went to work full-time dressing department-store mannequins. Upon marrying her husband Phil in 1982, she turned her fashion sense toward home and family, which eventually included daughters Amanda and Katrina. Soon Nicol was making dried-flower wreaths, taking them to crafts shows, and sewing stuffed cloth dolls to complement her displays.

By 1989, she was making about twenty signed and numbered Santa dolls a year for a local gift shop called Close to Home (no longer in business). Nicol credits the owner, Judy Guerino, for encouraging her to continue. Retailing at the time for $130 to $200 each, the dolls brought extra income that was especially welcome at Christmastime.

TAKING FLIGHT

At the time, Nicol was making her Santa faces from polymer clay, which she says was an improvement over her previous flat cloth faces. The only problem was that the weight of the clay often caused her figures to slouch. After researching alternate materials at crafts stores, she began to experiment with lighter-weight papier-mâché.

Today, her smaller papier-mâché dolls retail for $50 to $200, and they're "taking flight" in fifteen shops around the country. Larger dolls command $300 to $1,000, depending on their size, embellishments, and trim. When she's not making Santas, Nicol works on other historically inspired papier-mâché figures, as well as angels and pumpkin heads.

Nicol admits that her dolls have changed over the years. "They were more primitive in the beginning," she says. Although today's examples are more traditional, her signature use of vintage materials is a binding thread. "I'll continue to make Santas for as long as people continue to enjoy them." ✦

This wooden display case was made especially to showcase a Santa clad in robes of antique gold bullion trim and matching fringe.

This exquisite doll theater made from vintage paper is embellished with antique tinsel, metal ornaments, and crepe paper.

WINTER WISHES

Dressed in vintage garb, this Santa carries an antique cart filled with brush trees.

Opposite: "People like my dolls so much," Sharon says, "that they don't want just one—they want multiples. That's a great compliment." At age forty-seven, she feels her dollmaking career is just beginning.

For Goodness' Sake

THESE SPLENDID SHARON ANDREWS SANTAS INSPIRE GOODNESS AT EVERY TURN.

Sharon Andrews and her family live in the house that dolls built. Hundreds of spirited Santa figures have come alive within its walls. They've become Sharon's livelihood and her love, and they've turned her one-thousand-square-foot basement in Columbus, Ohio, into a veritable Santa's workshop.

Although twenty years of crafting have given her a definitive style, Sharon says her Santa dolls still enjoy broad appeal. Some collectors see them as primitive, others say they look Victorian, and still others applaud their French Provincial manner. With their humble eyes, modest midlines, and resplendent holiday robes, these Santas are hard not to love.

ONE-OF-A-KIND CHARACTERS

Constructed of wire, wood, and sculpted cloth, each Sharon Andrews doll evolves as magically as the legend himself. "I used to wonder," Sharon says, "'What if I

run out of ideas?'" But she's since discovered that the more she works, the more ideas she generates.

Sharon's greatest joy is in designing one-of-a-kind Santas, each with his own unique expression. A crazy-quilt scrap may inspire one figure just as surely as a shiny piece of hardware sparks another. "I don't see anything for what it really is," she says. A twenty-year antiques-show and flea-market veteran, Sharon is adept at spotting the potential in throwaways.

She accessorizes her jolly old men with antique embellishments from her profuse collections of glass Victorian beads, old pocket watches, miniature pinecones, and countless other ornaments. If necessary, she may add a reproduction feather tree or a hand-sculpted snowman to complete her vision.

"My characters look a little like me," Sharon says, referring to her Santas' facial contours and high cheekbones. She begins by molding each face from

Written by Judith Stern Friedman ✦ *Photographs by Jeff Ricus*

fabric painted with gesso or from Creative Paperclay (available at crafts stores). After rounding the shape and sculpting the cheekbones, she dabs on features with acrylic paints. The beards are recycled sheep's wool, which Sharon glues or stitches in place. The hands often are fabric mittens, she explains, "because my Santas usually have so many things to hold."

SPREADING JOY

Although many artists are reluctant to reveal their secrets, Sharon is happy to share hers. (To re-create one of her folk-art Santas, see *page 138*.) "I believe in giving," she says, "because so many people have encouraged me along the way." The daughter of a frequently transferred electrical engineer, Sharon thinks of western Tennessee as her childhood home.

Above: To fabricate Santa's costumes, Sharon sometimes cuts up antique quilts (but only if they're already irreparably damaged). She also uses velvet costumes, curtains, paisleys, brocades, old Indian camp blankets, feed sacks, and linen.

"My parents were always making things," she says. One Christmas when she opened a box from her mother filled with handmade doll clothes, she immediately knew that she wanted to make such wonderful things herself.

By age eight, Sharon had learned to embroider; by the ninth grade, she'd sewn a fully lined maxi-coat. Then sewing took a backseat until after high school. Sharon married and began a family of her own, including children Camille, Nikki, and Tyler. When the children were young in the early 1980s, Sharon's husband Art bought her a sewing machine for Christmas.

Soon she was designing children's clothes, smocked pillows, rag dolls, and other fabric-inspired crafts. "People just wanted to buy them," Sharon says. Then when her family moved to Ohio in 1983, she discovered that most women didn't have the time to make these kinds of things. But because they had jobs outside the home, they did have disposable income. Sharon saw that she could fill a need and began doing crafts shows across eight midwestern states.

Sharon hand-signs each one-of-a-kind Santa doll, adding value to the original pieces, which now retail for $360 to $1,200. Her imported versions, unsigned, sell for $20 to $80, but they make her art accessible to a broader audience.

*Ranging in size from twelve to
twenty-nine inches, these Santas
incorporate flea-market finds
and homemade cornucopias
copied from old sheet music.*

JUMP-STARTED SUCCESS

In 1989, a friend, Patty Rauss, convinced Sharon to show her wares at the wholesale folk-art market in Valley Forge, Pennsylvania. "I made holiday-themed dolls people had never seen before," she explains. Just hours before she was to leave for the show, she still hadn't finished two new designs she'd started: two twelve-inch Father Christmas dolls dressed in old quilts. She pushed herself to add the final touches and left for the show with the Santas in tow, never dreaming that the dolls would change her life.

This Santa was inspired by a medallion from an old costume and a chenille star that reminded Sharon of Christmas decorations from her childhood. A handmade cotton-batting tree complements the finished piece.

Sharon's last-minute instincts were right on target: The first visitor to her booth, a dealer from New York, placed an order for 150 Santa dolls. At that show alone, she received $38,000 worth of orders—more than she'd sold in the previous three years combined. To meet this sudden demand, she started a cottage industry of fifteen neighborhood moms who worked as seamstresses. The following year, sales doubled. "I was making as many Santas as I could physically handle twelve months out of the year," Sharon recalls.

By January 2000, the volume and repetition had begun to take their toll. "I had become a production manager when I wanted to be a designer," Sharon says. So she disbanded the cottage industry save for one design assistant and went back to creating elaborate one-of-a-kinds. But the marketplace wouldn't let her scale back quite so easily. In March 2000, the owner of ESC Trading Company approached her about reproducing her Santas overseas. Although reluctant at first, Sharon eventually became convinced that if she didn't take this step, others would copy her work. By March 2001, twelve different Sharon Andrews designs were smiling down from the shelves at the Atlanta International Wholesale Gift Show.

A HAPPY LANDING

Although Sharon insists that one-of-a-kind Santas are her true passion, mass merchandising has allowed her to expand her business to include pillows, place mats, table runners, and even a line of furniture. Earning royalties from her designs has eased the pressure and given her more freedom to create.

Today, Sharon continues to sell her vintage Santas, imported pieces, and whatever new products she might imagine. She still owns many of her original Santas but recently put them in storage for her children. "Now I'm surrounded by my jars of ornaments and all the things that inspire," she says. This elf's work is never done, but as long as she can make people smile, she considers it all worthwhile. ✦

In Search of the Perfect Santa

LOIS CLARKSON MAKES SURE HER SANTA FIGURES ALWAYS
INCLUDE A SECRET INGREDIENT— A TWINKLE IN THEIR EYES.

Necessity, as they say, is the mother of invention. Pennsylvania Santa Claus-artist Lois Clarkson learned that the creative way.

"As a collector of antique toys, I've long been fascinated with old German papier-mâché candy containers, even though I knew I couldn't afford them," Lois explains. "I tried to duplicate them with papier-mâché that I made, but it was such a mess to work with."

When she finally tried polymer clay, the results were much better and her Santa career was born. Everything came together, she says. "I was an elementary-school teacher, but I'd always wanted to be an artist. So I combined my love of old toys, Santa Claus postcards, and art, and my life 'began' at age 45. I found what I wanted to be when I grew up."

SAVING FACE

By using German hand-blown glass eyes and duplicating images from travel books, Lois was able to give her figures much more lifelike faces. She found that European travel books and brochures were a bonanza, and she especially enjoys duplicating their characters, right down to the rosy cheeks, bulbous noses, and fluffy eyebrows.

"Faces can be a challenge," Lois points out. "My inspiration is different for each one. I even used former President Jimmy Carter once." Portrait Santas

Written by Carol McGarvey ✦ *Photographs by Randy Foulds*

How Lois Clarkson adds a twinkle in the eyes of her Santa Claus figures is her secret, but it never fails to delight her clients.

Opposite: *After much experimentation, Lois settled on polymer clay as the perfect medium for achieving the special look of her Santa faces.*

are particularly hard, as she discovered when she completed one for a friend, Bob Phillips, who plays Santa in her area. To make the task even more daunting, Lois put Bob's real-life granddaughter on his knee.

Lois's husband, Jim, helps make the wooden torsos for many of her Santas, and he played an integral part in creating her studio. "Jim works in historic restoration in Bucks County, so our home is in three sections, like a lot of the area's old farmhouses," Lois explains. "There's the main section made of old thick stone from an earlier farmstead, plus a frame section and a log section." Her studio is in the log structure—perfect surroundings for a working artist.

Lois's Santas range from a diminutive 16 inches all the way to life-size, the latter of which are constructed in three parts to make them easier to ship. Because of the size differences, Lois never knows how long it will

A determined Father Christmas is a man on a mission to deliver toys and greetings for the approaching holiday.

Wool from a neighbor's llamas turns into wonderful beards for Lois's Santas. She carefully searches for antique toys in just the right scale for her Santas' packs.

take to make each one. "Some days I'm in a 'head mood,' and all I'll do is heads."

Besides her standing figures, Lois also makes Santas that sit on vintage-style sleds. Altogether, she makes about forty new Santas each year. "I tend to work in spurts," she admits, "but sometimes I become a hermit when the work is all-consuming."

TWO STYLES OF SANTAS

Lois fashions her Santas' beards from a neighbor's llama wool or from purchased wool ends. She shops often for antique toys for her figures that carry bags, checking that the scale is right for each one since they range so in size. When she looks for vintage velvets for her cloaks, she must be careful to choose only old fabrics that are still stable enough to use. Although she does at least one show each year, her work is known primarily by word of mouth among collectors, who are happy to pay anywhere from $400 to $3,000 for each piece.

When you buy a Santa from Lois, you have your choice of two different styles. "First, there's the European Father Christmas look like my French Père Noël, with his long robes and picking basket," she says. The second type is the 1950s version from Lois's childhood. "They're always cheery, unlike some of their European counterparts such as Belsnickles, who carried sticks to punish misdeeds."

At one show, Lois relates, a French woman came up to her and said, "Oh, that's exactly the Father Christmas of my childhood. Our grandfather always

Right: *Lois's 1950s-era Santas always sport a cherry smile and a twinkle in their eyes.*

Opposite: *Her other style of Santa is more European, resembling an English Father Christmas or a French Père Noël, complete with long robes and a picking basket.*

had us look up the chimney to the stars. He would say the stars were under the cape of Father Christmas." So now Lois always puts stars on the linings of those figures' cloaks.

Christmas was a magical, homey, and wonderful holiday in Lois's youth. "My mother once gave me an old train set just like the one I'd had as a little girl. Suddenly I could still smell the smells and feel the feelings of those Christmases of long ago."

With tongue firmly in cheek, Lois named her business and work space Snowdin Studios. "Many people believe it's a real name and want to know the origin. It's easy," she says with a chuckle. "It stands for 'snowed in,' as in the winter. And sometimes in the fall when I have lots of work to finish, it could just as easily be called 'snowed under.'" ✦

A Collector's Passion

TREASURES FROM CHRISTMAS PAST

ADD CHARM TO THE NEW SANTA FIGURES WEST VIRGINIA

ARTIST PAUL GORDON LOVINGLY CREATES.

Above: *In his studio of nine small rooms, Paul Gordon organizes his Santa supplies. Here he rearranges shelves of colorful quilt blocks and fabric swatches.*

Opposite: *Paul's studio is full of holiday inspiration. Surrounded by old toys and trims, he relies on the spirit of Christmas Past to shape his modern-day creations.*

Becoming a pack rat at an early age has served Santa Claus artist Paul Gordon well. He still takes great delight in removing the batting from old quilts, scouring tag sales and flea markets for vintage trims, and searching out jars of discarded buttons—all in the service of his modern-day Santa dolls.

"My Santa, snowman, and garden figures are part of the whole process, my whole artistic evolution," Paul explains. The former wedding-gown designer and tailor also has worked in the field of textile restoration, so he brings a strong sense of history to his creations.

His work with Santas began about sixteen years ago when he wanted to purchase some antique Santa ornaments for his Christmas tree. Taken aback by their high cost, he considered making his own. It was only

Written by Carol McGarvey ✦ *Photographs by Randy Foulds*

Passersby are charmed by Paul's year-round approach to Christmas. It's hard to resist the welcome extended by the seasonal pieces outside his workshop.

Paul delights in creating whimsical characters with a droll look and overstated eyes.

when he fashioned a bunny out of old wool blankets for a baby gift and an admirer asked him to make a Santa doll that he decided to give it a try. Soon friends were offering to buy his Santas, and his cottage industry was off and running.

HEADS UP!

Interestingly shaped gourds from a Thanksgiving centerpiece became the heads of his first whimsical characters and the foundation for the sculpted-clay faces with their huge eyes. Word-of-mouth buzz and Paul's participation in a Washington, D.C., farmer's market ignited sales.

"Because each gourd is different, each Santa figure is different," the artist explains. "For my garden sculptures, any item—a teapot or a watering can—has the potential to become the head."

When his 1870s home in Martinsburg, West Virginia, began to look more like a North Pole workshop, Paul knew it was time to move his business to a dedicated studio. That's also when he stumbled upon a former antiques shop that was available and immediately decided that its nine tiny rooms would be perfect for bringing some semblance of order to all his found materials. The shop even had a bay window, which to the delight of passersby has become a showcase for Paul's creative seasonal displays.

Although a big worktable is the focal point of the studio, the warren of rooms is the real workhorse. Some rooms are stacked floor-to-ceiling with old quilts; others are lined with shelves of clear plastic bins full of

Interestingly shaped gourds magically become the heads of holiday characters with expressive eyes. An hour-glass Santa holds a bag of toys in one hand and a feather tree and colorful beads in the other.

Although many of Paul's figures have solemn faces, this rosy-cheeked example exudes the spirit of the season.

Opposite: *A Santa gift giver holds the reins of his goose-head sleigh, full of toy-size animals. His expressive eyes, homespun garb, and red gloves make him a standout.*

buttons, trims, and ribbons. One room is nothing but Easter baskets; another is home to Paul's ever expanding stash of fabrics. Paul even has the luxury of separate rooms for painting and woodcutting.

The inspiration for Paul's Santas often comes from his collection of antique children's books and old postcards, which he says are peopled with characters whose sweet facial expressions just beg to be seen once again. If one of his jolly old men happens to be carrying a bag, Paul insists that it be stuffed with authentic antique toys, which he ferrets out at sales

and flea markets. (Friends and acquaintances have even gotten into the habit of bringing him their vintage finds when they clean out their attics and basements.) As a finishing touch, he sprinkles his figures with mica dust for a bit of added sparkle right in keeping with the magic of the season.

PLAYING FAVORITES

The resulting Santas range in height from 10 inches all the way to 7 feet and take Paul anywhere from two days to three weeks to complete. Priced at $55 to $4,000 each, they're marketed by small galleries and boutiques and sold directly to loyal collectors who return year after year. Is it ever hard to let a favorite piece leave the studio? Absolutely, Paul says, "but collectors become my friends so I always have visiting rights." Indeed, as a collector himself, he'd rather search out extraspecial Santas and snowmen from other artists than hold on to his own pieces.

"Collectors want Santas and snowmen no matter what the season. They don't just put them out at the holidays. Amazingly, most of my snowmen go to the West Coast," Paul says. "Many transplants from colder climates have a nostalgic attachment to winter, and they display the figures all year."

Although his work invariably leaves him exhausted by the time Christmas arrives, Paul still manages to put up several decorated feather trees in his home. "Christmas has always been special to me. We lived in a rural area for a time when I was a child, and we cut our own tree. I learned handcrafts from my grandmother. She taught me how to sew, knit, and to make collages." Needless to say, Paul is proud that her legacy lives on in his sweetly sentimental Santas. ✦

Whimsical Wonders

WHAT IS IT ABOUT THESE VICTORIAN FATHER CHRISTMAS DOLLS THAT GIVES THEM THE POWER TO REKINDLE PRECIOUS CHILDHOOD MEMORIES?

Above: *Recognized by* Early American Life *magazine as one of America's "200 Top Craftsmen," Yvonne Carpenter is casting a fresh, new glow on an old tradition. She also was invited to design a Christmas ornament for the 1999 White House Christmas tree.*

Opposite: *Yvonne casts her Santa faces and boots using hydrostone molds she makes in her basement. The curly mohair beard can take as long as two hours to glue on because it has to hang just right.*

It's no wonder that Yvonne Carpenter's five grandchildren, all under seven years old, look forward to visiting Grandma's house. No ordinary home, it's more like a year-round Christmas pageant: A marionette mocks a grinning jester, a playful pig totters on a rocking horse, and woolly sheep "baaa" at all the silly antics. Especially at Christmastime (which for Yvonne starts the day after Halloween), Father Christmas dolls of every shape and size bring delight to this gingerbread house, an 1878 Victorian beauty in Haddonfield, New Jersey.

The children find it hard not to reach out and touch these lifelike heroes, with their bushy beards, velvety robes, and armfuls of vintage toys. But it's these merry men who have touched so many others. They may be

Written by Judith Stern Friedman ✦ *Photographs by Randy Foulds*

reminiscent of their German and English forebears, but these dolls are forging new traditions right here in America.

PIECES OF THE PAST

"I started this business so I could enjoy Christmas twelve months a year," Yvonne says. Her company's name, Snickles and Kringles, says a lot about her creative spirit. "I love whimsy," she says, which is evident in every detail, all the way down to the charming toys she creates for each of her Father Christmas dolls to hold.

Inspired by the time-honored creations of German toymakers, Yvonne seeks to recapture the spirit of the 1800s. When she can't find authentic antique toys, she reproduces them herself using fabric, basswood, and composition (a mix of plaster, glue, and paper pulp)— the same materials craftsmen would have used two centuries ago. For example, her signature sheep designs preserve the German putz tradition of displaying village scenes under the Christmas tree. Yvonne casts their bodies, carves the legs, and even dyes recycled lamb's wool to use for their pelts.

Just as with her finely detailed toys, Yvonne also lavishes attention on the dolls themselves. The hardest part is creating the right expression, she says. That often requires multiple tries at sculpting the face in clay and making a master mold from hydrostone. Finally she casts the faces in composition (which could take up to a week to dry) and adds finishing touches with acrylic paints. Any given mold could last for twenty to thirty castings before Yvonne has to retire it; however, she now produces only a few faces from each one to establish her collectible limited editions.

For each body, she builds a wire-and-wood armature, which she then wraps in billowy batting. Next she designs the gentleman's garb, usually velvet or brocade trimmed with recycled mink or chinchilla fur. If she can't find vintage fabric, she dyes new material until it

Yvonne keeps all her original Santa prototypes, displaying some on her parlor mantel and giving others to her children. Whenever possible, she uses authentic materials and construction techniques, such as the mica "snow" she grinds by hand.

looks suitably aged. She also cuts apart old leather gloves to warm Santa's hands for his worldly flight.

VICTORIAN VISION

Yvonne's Victorian home of more than twenty-five years is a fitting backdrop for her sprawling antique collections. Since moving here in 1976, she's amassed enough old toys, ornaments, tinsel, and holiday memorabilia to adorn eight trees throughout her home. Nearly every Saturday, she shuttles off to the Berlin Farmer's Market, where she searches out new treasures to add to her displays. Her most recent prizes

are the cast-iron benches she hopes to eventually include in a putz.

"My house is highly decorated," Yvonne readily admits. Brimming with ornaments for show as well as work in progress, the place is a menagerie of happy characters. Counters are covered with her smiling Vinterkinder, or snow children; the dining-room table is a runway of Santa suits; and the living room doubles as an assembly line of wool, sheep's legs, and other doll parts.

Yvonne describes her third-floor studio as an "inspirational workroom" that's perpetually decorated with the tools of her trade. "It's a place I love to go," she says. When her dolls aren't on display throughout the house, they come home to this haven to relax among the lights and animated toys, boxes of baubles and beads, and caches of old Christmas books and postcards.

"Ideas just come to me," Yvonne says, admitting that some of them seem downright silly. She may be sleeping or relaxing when she envisions a scene, which she later sketches to define the details. She also looks forward to the annual Golden Glow Convention (a worldwide meeting of Santa fans and collectors) in July, where she meets kindred spirits who share her love of Santa.

Whenever possible, Yvonne uses authentic materials and construction techniques to give her Santas an old-world look.

Opposite: *These majestic Santas seem to almost come to life while standing next to this wintry-looking hearth.*

CASTING OFF

An artist by training, Yvonne credits her education with helping her work evolve but says it's sheer trial and error that accounts for her success. "The more you do, the more you improve," she says. Still, dollmaking comes naturally to her—her mother actually ran a doll hospital. By age eleven, she'd learned to sew and was already stitching her own clothes.

After graduating in the first art class at Glassboro State College (now Rowan University) in Glassboro, New Jersey, Yvonne married her husband, Tom (now a retired college counselor), and taught grade-school art for two years until her first son, Andy, was born in 1968. Then she was lucky enough to stay home, spending the next eighteen years raising three more children—Kelly, Casey, and Karey—and promoting various handmade crafts with a friend at gift shows. Finally she honed in on the German-influenced holiday dolls and miniatures that have become her trademark.

By 1986, her dolls (and her house) had landed on the pages of a national magazine, drawing an over-whelming five hundred orders for her distinctive sheep. Although the magazine feature and wholesale gift shows continued to bring in orders for the next fourteen years, the work became all-consuming.

In 2001, Yvonne finally opted out of her demanding schedule and scaled back to holding just one show out of her home each year, open by invitation only to one hundred friends and family members. She continues to sell sheep and goats by direct mail and through a few loyal shops but no longer actively pursues new business.

Her one-of-a-kind Father Christmas dolls now retail for $800 to $1,000 each, and the orders have continued despite a tough economy. As *The Nutcracker Suite* serenades her and Christmas lights twinkle all around, Yvonne's eyes sparkle with a special glow because she's immersed in the work she loves. ✦

Papier-mâché roly-poly dolls stand from six to twelve inches tall. The small lantern at left below, meant to hang in front of a bulb or window, has translucent paper behind the eyes and mouth.

Opposite: *Nyla Murphy is flanked by a doll-type Belsnickle on her right and a bobble-head Santa on her left.*

Born-Again Belsnickles

SAINT NICHOLAS FIGURES FROM THE LATE NINETEENTH CENTURY COME
TO LIFE IN THE HANDS OF A MICHIGAN CRAFTER WHOSE SCULPTED AND
PAINTED SANTAS QUALIFY AS INSTANT HEIRLOOMS.

In her charming 1871 Victorian home in the village of Milford, Michigan, Nyla Murphy turns papier-mâché into German-inspired Belsnickles that are snapped up by eager collectors. She does not attend crafts shows or exhibit in galleries. Her business is strictly word of mouth, and it keeps her busy full-time—with overtime at Christmas.

Nyla was supposed to be born on Christmas Day. Her mother even had picked out the perfect name: Christine Carol. But Nyla didn't make her appearance until two weeks later and so received a decidedly non-holiday name. But that hasn't stopped her: For the past two decades, she's worked day in and day out sculpting and painting the papier-mâché Santa figures known as Belsnickles, or "Nicholas in fur."

Belsnickles, which were made in Germany from the 1870s until 1917, are hollow papier-mâché figures that are cast in a two-piece mold, front and back, and then seamed together and painted. Typically, they're Father Christmas characters with clasped hands hidden in the sleeves of a cloak. A tree made from goose feathers dyed green often is tucked in the crook of one arm.

STICKER SHOCK

It was a long-ago visit to an antiques shop that prompted Nyla's foray into Belsnickles. Although she'd seen vintage versions in magazines and had always thought collecting them would be fun, it was only after much fruitless searching that she found an authentic six-inch Belsnickle for sale. The price was $400, far

Written by Allison Engel ✦ *Photographs by Perry Struse*

more than she was willing to spend. "And here I wanted to collect a whole bunch of them!" she recalls with a laugh.

She told a friend that she wished someone would make reproduction Belsnickles that people could actually afford. Her friend, knowing Nyla's skill at oil painting, suggested that person might be *her*.

Nyla rose to the challenge and developed a construction method that she prefers to keep mostly secret. She shuns ready-made molds, preferring to sculpt her Belsnickles from clay or papier-mâché. She then makes a plaster mold and casts the figures with more papier-mâché. The two halves are seamed together, left to dry, and then painted. Sometimes she sprinkles on little flakes of mica to suggest new-fallen snow.

Nyla's figures range in size from five to eighteen inches tall and sell for $35 to $325 each. For $650, you can buy one of her bobble-head Santas with a rabbit-fur beard and a wool-felt costume. Other Santas come apart at the waist to hold candy, just like the 1890s

This Santa riding a spotted pig holds a leather bridle and whip and carries a basket of greenery on his back. The 8^1/$_2$-inch figure sells for $200.

Above: *White Belsnickles line a mantel in Nyla's bedroom amid flasks of perfume. They range in size from six to fourteen inches tall.*

Nyla displays a bevy of Belsnickles on an old cupboard in her "Santa room," which features a hand-stenciled wall.

German originals that inspired them. Nyla also sculpts large three-dimensional Santa faces, which become statement-making focal points when hung on a wall. To give her pieces the patina of age, she dyes the wool felt for her costumes and make judicious use of muted paint colors and old-world designs.

BY APPOINTMENT ONLY

You won't find these sought-after collectibles at crafts shows or galleries. The only place Nyla displays her wares is in the showroom she maintains in her home. Its custom-built scaled-down fireplace mantel is lined with Belsnickles and painted chalkware cats—another of her specialties. Customers make appointments, see what's on display, and then order their pieces in the sizes and styles they prefer. No two of Nyla's figures are alike. "I'll do different sizes or faces or vary the way they stand," she says. "I have to keep coming up with new ideas because I have customers who collect one of everything I make."

This mother of three grown children admits that she's a perfectionist and says she stays fresh by making only what interests her. The source of her inspiration: her collection of old books on European Christmas traditions. "I thought it would take the joy out of Christmas for me to work with it all year, but I still love Christmas and decorate madly for the holidays," Nyla says. Orders do get backed up in November and December, though. "Sometimes I'll stay up until 1 a.m. and then get up at 5," she admits. "I get in that work mode and don't want to quit."

No matter what the season, Nyla's customers love to keep her figures on constant display. "A lot of people leave them out all year, even though they're holiday decorations," she says. "They do look nice with antiques." ✦

These bobble-head Belsnickles and candy-container Belsnickles sport handmade clothing stitched from fabric that Nyla dyes and fades to look old.

Telling Tales

WITH FIGURES SO REALISTIC YOU COULD SWEAR THEY ALMOST MOVE, SUSAN McMULLEN CREATES VIGNETTES THAT BRING CHRISTMAS STORIES TO LIFE.

Above: Enthralled by the kindly spirit of Santa Claus at an early age, Susan McMullen—now grown up, inset—makes an art of capturing his likeness in polymer clay.

Opposite: Exquisitely detailed scenes from Susan's imagination take form in elaborate vignettes that often are based on her own childhood memories.

It was more than the first-time jitters. To hear Canadian artist Susan McMullen tell it, heading off to her first crafts fair made her so nervous she could hardly exhibit the ornamental figures she had made. She needn't have worried. The eager customers were enthralled by her clever salt-dough characters— especially her Santas—and her booth sold out in under an hour.

Encouraged by this success, Susan decided to develop her talent for sculpting. "Since the Santas were my most popular figures, I concentrated on them," she says. "I've always been a nut about Christmas, but who could have imagined that I'd build a whole career on Santa Claus!"

Susan quickly realized that salt dough wasn't permanent enough for her art, and she switched to polymer clay. "My first order was for two hundred

Written by Shelley Stewart ✦ *Photographs by Perry Struse*

pounds of clay, and I was able to make five heads," she says. "I had to buy enough clay so I would have some left if my first tries failed. I always say you should never be afraid to fail because each time you do, you'll learn something from it. And I had a lot to learn!" With the pliable clay, Susan found she could capture far more detail than with salt dough, and soon her figures became much more three-dimensional.

LEARNING BY DOING

Creating lifelike Santa dolls went from craft to passion. Susan took a sculpting class but decided that if she were to become a real expert, she'd have to learn by doing. "I also bought every dollmaking video I could find," she adds, "and I found at least one good idea in each one."

After much trial and error, Susan finally hit on the perfect clays to use for sculpting: Prosculpt for her Santas because it produces such fine detail and a 60/40 mix of Cernit and Sculpey for children's figures because it creates such a delicate porcelainlike

complexion. Never one to rely on standard methods, she also developed her own unique system for mixing the clays. "I put chunks of both types of clay inside doubled plastic freezer bags and warm them slightly by standing the bags in a sink of hot water. Then I step on the bags to mix the clay," she says.

But the secret to making her figures look so lifelike isn't in the clay. "The key is to bend the wire armature so the figure seems to be moving," Susan says. "I sculpt the head and the feet before I get the armature on its feet. Only then do I sculpt the hands—after I bend the armature into its final position. That's how I make them look so realistic."

Above: Susan sculpts each Santa face with wrinkles, natural skin tones, and a unique expression, adding a silky mohair beard and hair for even more realism.

Opposite: Small details such as the difference between younger and older skin textures are characteristic of Susan's sculptures. She uses a special mix of clays to capture the dewy complexions of children.

Although Susan's first dolls were just 24 inches tall, most now are larger—up to 50 inches tall. "I love to do the bigger figures," she says. "If you have a lovely house, a really large Santa beside the fireplace or tree creates a bit of magic. You almost want to go up and cuddle the guy."

SETTING THE SCENE

Susan wasn't content to stop at making the most lifelike dolls many Santa collectors had ever seen. She went on to create entire vignettes—small scenes that include her Santas alongside other characters. Each vignette wordlessly tells a Christmas story, down to the smallest detail. Santa may be checking his list at a desk surrounded by elves, or he might be tenderly leaning over to kiss a sleeping baby. Each figure is as accurate

This freestanding Santa is actually simpler than most of Susan's pieces, despite its elaborate fur-trimmed costume, lace-up boots, and pack of toys.

and realistic as Susan can make it, and she props her scenes with everything necessary to carry out the illusion. Depending on the theme, she might include miniature toys and books, furry animals and feathered birds, or child-size chairs and hand-carved tables.

Susan often draws inspiration for her vignettes from the luscious silk velvets and brocades that eventually grace her dolls. "A lot of times, a wonderful fabric will set me off and I'll design the whole Santa around it," she says. "There's an import shop here in Vancouver that brings in fabrics from all over the world." After loading up a bag with an assortment of finds, she'll share sketches and her latest ideas with longtime friend and collaborator, master seamstress Madalyn Doyon. Together, they might spend hours planning the construction of garments for the next vignette.

The clothing you see is only the beginning—each doll's garb also includes carefully made inner garments and underwear. Santa might well be wearing a silk charmeuse shirt adorned with antique lace beneath his fur-trimmed velvet robe.

The flowing white beard and silky hair are so integral to her Santas that Susan uses only mohair shorn from Angora goats raised on a local farm. Before creating the hair for her other figures, she carefully dyes the mohair and then styles it with hair curlers once the hair is in place. "The diameter of each mohair strand is smaller than a human hair, and that makes it perfect for dolls," she explains.

These details, together with the astounding realism of her sculpting, are all it takes to convince serious collectors to invest in Susan's Santa vignettes. Sometimes a collector will special-order a figure with hair and eyes to match those of a particular child, and Susan is happy to oblige. But she insists that her most exciting work happens when she brings life to Santa by following her own artistic vision. "The challenge is to see if I can create what I'm imagining," she says, "and for me the best part is the 'zing' of seeing it finished." ◆

Incorporating "props" that help set the stage, every vignette tells its own story. Multiple characters and sometimes even animals get into the act.

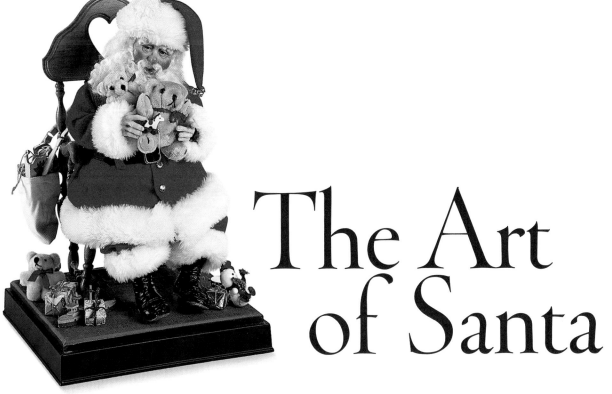

The Art of Santa

IN LITTLE MORE THAN A DECADE, JACK JOHNSTON
OF SALT LAKE CITY HAS BECOME THE PIED PIPER OF ART DOLLS.
HIS FAVORITE SUBJECT? SANTA CLAUS, OF COURSE.

Above: *One of Jack's early Santas,
circa 1993, sits alongside stuffed
bears and a pouch full of toys.*

Opposite: *Dollmaker Jack Johnston and
his wife Vicky, the vice president of his
doll company, pose with Jack's Alter Ego
Santa, a life-size, totally posable doll
that took him a full month to make.*

Before the four books, seven videos, the two million flight miles to teach classes, the huge booth at the American International Toy Fair in New York City, the magazine covers, and the seven-thousand-square-foot gallery and academy, Jack Johnston's dollmaking empire consisted only of a single Santa Claus he'd made to give at Christmas because he was broke.

It was 1990, and Jack had recently lost his job as a marketing executive. With six children to support, times were tough—worse than tough. As Jack recalls, "We were stone broke. And we had a son with leukemia and no health insurance." That Christmas, Jack's wife had a modest request: All she wanted was a Santa Claus doll.

Jack, who had a degree in commercial art, bought some clay, doll's hair, and clothing. His initial effort

Written by Allison Engel ✦ *Photographs by Ed Gohlich*

turned out reasonably well, so he asked his wife if he could try to sell the doll at a local crafts show. She agreed, and he priced it at $129. He not only sold that Santa but ended up taking orders for eight more. Jack decided then and there that his future would be in dolls. One week later, he attended another crafts show, pricing his Santas at $299. He was even more successful, taking orders for more than a dozen. Two weeks later, he raised the price to $499. That first year in business, he sold more than two hundred dolls.

A CAREER IS BORN

Today, Jack's dolls are in private collections and museums worldwide, and command an average price of $2,000. But one doll, a three-dimensional rendering of artist Norman Rockwell's famed triple self-portrait, was sold to the Franklin Mint for $30,000. That sale was a career highlight for Jack, who has admired Norman Rockwell from the age of eight. Growing up on a farm outside Dodge City, Kansas, without any electricity, he wasn't able to listen to the radio or watch television as a child. But he could read *The Saturday Evening Post* and study Rockwell's cover art. Those expressive, detailed figures that tell a story with their body language, clothing, and accessories are echoed in the eighteen- to twenty-inch dolls that Jack crafts today.

"I try to put a story in each of my sculptures," the artist explains. "It doesn't have to be an elaborate vignette." He pauses to think of an example. "Picture a Santa Claus. He's sitting on a chair with his legs thrown

Here are four of Jack's more recent dolls, ranging in height from eleven to eighteen inches. A small elf gazes at a teddy-bear craftsman as a Santa holding a carved wooden teddy bear looks on. At right is a bushy-bearded "master elf" adjusting his eyeglasses.

Jack believes that his Santas love toys as much as children do. This Santa is in his "off-season" wardrobe.

up, slippers on, and wearing red flannel PJs. There's a book on his lap that says '2002 Complete.' He's worn out but happy."

Santa Claus has remained Jack's favorite character and accounts for about half of the dolls he creates.

Realistic hands are a hallmark of Jack's work, but achieving them wasn't easy. When he first began, he put mittens on his Santa figures because he wasn't proud of their hands. To overcome this deficiency, he studied the anatomy of hands and embarked on years of practice.

Jack regularly seeks out flea markets for used clothing and jewelry for his "art dolls," as he calls them. "Old shirts, old curtains, old furs—I look for anything gorgeous. I like to put a lot of jewelry on my Father Christmases." He carefully squirrels away his treasures on shelves in his studio. "I'm quite different from many artists in that I'm very well organized," he says. "My entire studio is spotless."

Jack's meteoric rise in the doll world didn't surprise anyone who knew him. From the very beginning, he thought big and was alert to market opportunities. Within weeks of deciding that dollmaking would be his career, he had written a marketing plan and was lining up national distributors. When he was dissatisfied with the quality of the clay he was getting, he developed his own brand, ProSculpt polymer clay. And when he had trouble finding quality accessories, he started his own mail-order company to supply them. The longer he remained in business, the more unmet needs he noticed. Dollmaking books were in limited supply, so he wrote his own. He also developed an easy-to-use armature, or doll skeleton, that he had manufactured

Above: *Once his nemesis, carefully detailed hands are now a Johnston trademark.*

Opposite: *This life-size Santa has teeth that are hand-sculpted from translucent clay as well as blown-glass eyes that are the same kind used at Madame Tussaud's. His suit is trimmed in mohair from Tibet.*

in bulk. His video and doll-supplies business now employs eight people, including his mother Jane and stepfather Bob, who make the armatures and doll body stockings. As vice president of his doll company, his wife Vicky also spends her life around dollmaking. In 2000, when he felt the need for a permanent home for his dollmaking classes, he built a $1 million academy in Salt Lake City that serves as his home, his gallery, and a teaching facility.

Still, Jack is on the road teaching classes fifty weeks out of the year. He also annually invites twelve advanced students to take a professional class with him and attend the Toy Fair in New York City. There, he exhibits his dolls along with others in The Professional Doll Makers Art Guild, an organization he founded in 1993 to recognize talented one-of-a-kind doll artists. There are now more than three hundred members.

Jack's Santa-making video, which shows how to build a Santa from a simple base of compressed foil, is detailed enough to give a rank amateur the confidence to try his method of sculpting and painting. But he's forever tinkering with his Santas, planning ever more realistic and elaborate versions. He's even developed a fully posable Santa with a steel armature that allows every single joint—knees, ankles, wrist, hips, elbows, neck, and so on—to move.

"I'll never get tired of working with Santa," Jack says. "There's no one who doesn't like Santa. Everybody who collects dolls has at least one in their collection." ✦

Above: *Jack pays careful attention to every detail when sculpting, which is why his Santas are so lifelike.*

Opposite: *Tools of the dollmaking trade, clockwise from top left: two colors of sculpting clay, a Johnston "3 in 1" tool, a detail tool, a crafts knife, two hand armatures, a thin detail brush, a flat-bristle brush, two pieces of metal tape, and one piece of brown paper tape.*

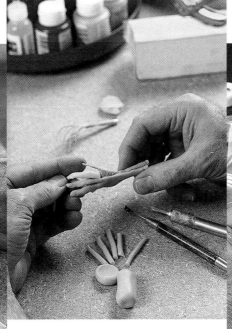

Santa's Hands

MATERIALS

- **Two hand armatures or a roll of 16-gauge copper wire**
- **Two brass tubes 3/16 inch in circumference**
- **Roll of aluminum plumber's tape**
- **Roll of floral tape**
- **ProSculpt polymer clay**
- **Sculpting tools**

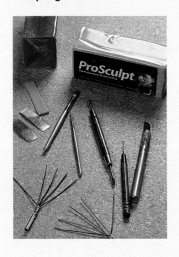

INSTRUCTIONS

Jack recommends making the hands after the head is completed in order to maintain the correct proportions.

Cut ten copper wires 2½ inches long for the fingers. Place five wires in each brass tube. Crimp the tubes to lock the wires in place. Spread the wires apart, and apply a piece of aluminum tape 1½ inches long by ½ inch wide over the base of four wires to hold them together. Using floral tape 15 inches long, wrap the tape around each brass tube from the bottom toward the palm. Stretch the tape, and wrap it around the wrist and the palm. Wrap the tape up the first finger, and tear it off when you reach the end. Wrap each finger by starting at the palm first. When all five fingers are wrapped, twist the paper on each finger so it fits snugly. Cut the wires to the desired length.

Make a thin roll of clay twice the length of each finger. Fold it in half and place it over a wire length. Smooth the seams on each side until the finger is secure at the base of the armature. Repeat for each finger.

Shape a piece of clay into a ball about the size of a small grape. Flatten the middle. This will form the palm of the hand. Lay the piece of clay at the base of the knuckles and against the inside of the thumb. Make a ball the size of a plum. Roll the ball into a cylinder shape about 1½ inches long. Cut the cylinder in half. Place the cylinder on the armature for the arm and wrist. Smooth all parts together to make the basic shape of the hand and arm. Cut excess clay from the bottom of the wrist up to the brass tube. Using a sculpting tool, form a ring around the base of the hand.

Using sculpting tools, begin to form the nail and knuckle shapes into the hand. Refer to the photos and real hands for placement. Repeat for the other hand.

Bake the hands according to the clay manufacturer's directions. See Sources on *page 158* for more information.

*Fanciful cards are a special way
to send holiday greetings through
the mail to family and friends.*

'Tis the season to deck your
home with holiday treasures!
Or create a holiday keepsake as a
gift for someone special.
Our unique Santa projects will
give you—and your recipients—
a joyously memorable holiday.

PERSONAL
EXPRESSIONS

Photograph by Greg Scheidemann

Santa Place Card

The card is 4⅝x3½ inches.

SANTA PLACE CARD MATERIALS

- **Anna Griffin Santa card (GC124) or any card with a Santa motif**
- **Burnisher or stylus**
- **Cutting mat**
- **Crafts knife**
- **Anna Griffin dark green patterned paper (AG051)**
- **Glue stick**
- **Computer and printer**
- **Sheet of ivory card stock**
- **Gold pen**
- **Ruler**
- **Adhesive-foam tape**

SANTA PLACE CARD INSTRUCTIONS

Cut a 4½-inch square from the card front with the Santa ⅛ inch from the left edge and ½ inch from the bottom edge. Use a burnisher or stylus to mark the horizontal center on the back of the square 2¼ inches below the top edge. Place the square on a cutting mat and use the crafts knife to carefully cut out the Santa above the burnish mark. Fold the square in half on the burnish mark, allowing the Santa to stand upright. Trim the irregularly cut edges on the back of the place card into a smooth curved line.

From the dark green paper, cut a ¼x4½-inch strip. Mount the strip along the bottom front edge of the place card using a glue stick.

To personalize the place card, use the computer to type the desired name to fit in a 2¼x⅜-inch area. Print a test sample. Adjust the font size if needed. When satisfied, print the name in black ink on the ivory card stock. Centering the name, trim the card stock into a ⅝x2½-inch strip. Use a gold pen and ruler to outline the edges and to draw a narrower outline just inside the outer outline. Mount the name strip on the place card using foam tape.

Designed by Jenna Beegle

Santa Card

The card is 7x5 inches.

SANTA CARD MATERIALS

- **Anna Griffin scrapbook papers: one sheet each of red, gold patterned, and red-and-gold patterned (AG025, AG027, and AG028)**
- **Purchased 5x7-inch blank ivory card**
- **Double-stick tape**
- **Anna Griffin Santa card (GC12224) or any card with a Santa motif**
- **Sheet of ivory card stock**
- **Embossing ink pen**
- **Gold embossing powder**
- **Embossing heat tool**
- **Adhesive-foam tape**

SANTA CARD INSTRUCTIONS

Cut a 6x4-inch rectangle of gold patterned paper. Center and mount the gold rectangle on the front of the blank ivory card with double-stick tape.

From the red paper, cut fifteen 1-inch squares. Referring to the photograph *opposite, left,* use double-stick tape to mount the red squares on the gold rectangle with corners touching to create a diamond pattern.

From the red-and-gold patterned paper, cut twelve 1-inch squares. Use foam tape to mount the red-and-gold squares on the diamond pattern, positioning the squares over the points where the red squares touch, as shown.

Centering the Santa motif, cut a 2¾x3¼-inch rectangle from the Santa card. Cut a 3x3½-inch rectangle of red paper and a 2x3¼-inch rectangle of ivory card stock. Use the embossing ink pen to apply ink to the edges of the Santa card rectangle. While the ink is wet, sprinkle it with gold embossing powder. Tilt the paper on edge and tap off the excess powder. Use the heat tool to melt the powder, creating a shiny raised image. Repeat to emboss the edges of the 3x3½-inch red rectangle, the 2x3¼-inch ivory rectangle, and the card.

Center and use double-stick tape to mount the Santa rectangle on the red rectangle and the red rectangle on the ivory rectangle. Mount the layered rectangles on the center of the card with foam tape.

Designed by Lynn Morgan

Poinsettia Santa Tag

The tag is 4½x6 inches.

MATERIALS

- **Anna Griffin die cuts: journaling captions and Santa**
- **Anna Griffin patterned scrapbook papers: one sheet each of green and poinsettia**
- **Circle cutter**
- **Double-stick tape**
- **Sheet of red card stock**
- **Pencil**
- **¼-inch hole punch**
- **1 yard length of Anna Griffin ⅞-inch-wide hunter green satin ribbon**

POINSETTIA SANTA TAG INSTRUCTIONS

Cut a 4-inch diameter journaling circle from the sheet of journaling caption die cuts. Use a circle cutter to cut a 3⅝-inch-diameter circle from the green patterned paper and a 3-inch-diameter circle from a Santa die cut.

Center and mount the Santa circle on the green circle with double-stick tape. To fringe the green circle, cut slits about ¹⁄₁₆ inch apart from the outer edge of the green paper to the edge of the Santa circle. Rub your fingertip over the cut edge of the green circle to add dimension to the fringe. Center and mount the layered circles on the journaling circle.

Cut an individual poinsettia from the poinsettia-patterned paper. Mount the layered circles on the bottom half of the poinsettia to complete the tag front.

Place the tag front on the red card stock. Lightly draw around the tag with a pencil and cut out just inside the drawn lines. Mount the tag front on the card stock shape. Use the ¼-inch hole punch to make a hole through the tag ½ inch below the center top. Cut a V in each end of the ribbon. Thread the ribbon through the hole and tie the ribbon ends in a bow.

Designed by Holle Wiktorek

See Sources, page 158.

Photograph by Greg Scheidemann

Casting Santa

THESE UNIQUE MOLDS
ARE WORKING REPLICAS
OF HISTORICAL COOKIE
MOLDS USED TO MAKE
SPRINGERLE COOKIES.

Photograph by Marty Baldwin

MATERIALS

- **Rolling pin**
- **Creative Paperclay air-drying modeling compound**
- **Paintable mist mold release**
- **The House on the Hill Santa molds: Santa with striped coat #2051, Santa with sack of toys #550, Father Christmas with tree #7001, deep Santa face #5855, large Santa with star #2029, and Santa with bag #5651**
- **Old knife**
- **Toothpick, dry ballpoint, or thin brush handle (to create hanging holes)**
- **Fine sandpaper**
- **Aleene's Mosaic Crackle Medium and Activator**
- **Assorted paintbrushes**
- **DecoArt Americana acrylic paints: Buttermilk #DA3, Antique White #DA58, Russet #DA80, Mississippi Mud #DA94, Shale Green #DA152, and Honey Brown #DA163**
- **Delta Ceramcoat Acrylic Paints: #2006 Avocado, #2518 Bahama Purple, #2490 Barn Red, #2506 Black, #2029 Caucasian Flesh, #2445 Green Sea , #2078 Straw, and #2038 Ultra Blue**
- **Plaid FolkArt Antiquing Medium #819**
- **Soft cloth**

   See Sources, page 158.

INSTRUCTIONS

With a rolling pin, roll out enough clay for one mold, smoothing it to ¼" thickness.

Spray a mold with paintable mist. Press the clay into the mold, adding more clay as necessary. Use the rolling pin to smooth the back of the mold if desired. Remove the clay from the mold. Trim and straighten the edges using a knife. If desired, push two holes in the top of the ornament for hanging. Set the mold aside to dry. *Note:* The clay will require two to three days of drying time. Watch the edges of the ornament for signs of curling, and push them back down onto the drying surface as needed. If the ornament dries with curled edges, simply hold it under running water until it's just wet, and press the shape back onto the drying surface. If cracks occur or you'd like to thicken an area, use thin layers of the clay to fill in the areas, smoothing them with the knife.

When the clay is dry, sand the edges and any rough surfaces.

To create a delicate crackled surface, mix one part crackle medium with two parts Buttermilk paint. (For a bolder effect, mix two parts of the medium with one part paint.) Paint the front and sides of the design with the mixture, and let it dry for 30 minutes.

Paint the design as desired. When the paint is dry, apply a coat of crackle-medium activator. Spread the activator over the entire design, or just brush areas where you'd like the crackled effect to appear. Set the ornament aside to crackle and dry. *Note:* The crackling won't appear until the activator begins to dry. You'll first notice the effect in areas where you've applied the activator the thinnest.

Using a small amount of antiquing medium and a soft cloth, apply and wipe off the medium, both at the same time. If the medium dries and the background is darker than you'd like, paint over the dark areas with Buttermilk paint (the crackling effect will still show through). Then simply repeat the antiquing process using a lighter touch. ✦

Designed by Laura Collins

House on the Hill is a small business located in Chicago that provides functional replicas of historical cookie molds. The molds are made of a resin-and-wood composite material and are copies of what were originally hand-carved wooden molds. Most of the original molds are from Europe, primarily Germany and Switzerland. House on the Hill molds are replicas of presses from both museums and private collections.

Many of the molds were family presses carved and handed down from generation to generation. Other molds were works commissioned by the very wealthy for specific events. Cookie molds are a fascinating piece of history and although they are functional, they are also beautiful to display.

Cotton-Batting Stockings

Finished stockings are 17 inches tall.

MATERIALS

For all stockings:

- **Pattern,** *page 133*
- **Pencil**
- **Tracing paper**
- **Straight-edge scissors**
- **Ruler**
- **Thin 100-percent cotton batting**
- **Steam iron and ironing board**
- **Matching sewing threads**
- **Sewing machine**
- **Old Print Factory Scrap Santa Claus motif or vintage scrap**
- **Spray adhesive**
- **Embroidery needle**
- **Straight pins**

For the Cuffed Stocking:

- **White dressmaker's pencil**
- **Three 8½×11-inch pieces of red felt**
- **Sandy Elliot's Christmas Bazaar flat, gold jingle bells (six ⅝-inch-wide and seven ½-inch-wide)**

For the Icicle-Trimmed Stocking:

- **Water-soluble marking pen**
- **D. Blümchen & Company items as follows: 19 inches of Eiszapfen-Fries icicles border; Old-Time Lametta tinsel garland**
- **Silver metallic thread**

For the Pinked-Edge Stocking:

- **Water-soluble marking pen**
- **Dressmaker's carbon paper**
- **Silver metallic thread**
- **D. Blümchen & Company items as follows: 55 inches of wide Lametta tinsel roping; 1-meter bag (39 inches) of real silver wide krausbouillion crinkle wire**
- **Pinking shears**
- **3½×5-inch piece of cardboard (an index card works well)**

CUFFED STOCKING

With a pencil, trace the outline of the stocking and cuff patterns, *page 137,* onto tracing paper. Also trace a separate toe and heel. Enlarge patterns 200 percent; cut out.

From cotton batting, cut out two stocking shapes. From one rectangle of red felt, cut out one toe, one heel, and a ½×5-inch hanging-loop strip. Stack the remaining two felt rectangles.

Using the dressmaker's pencil, draw the cuff shape on the top felt rectangle. Stitch the cuff sides, and then cut out the cuff, cutting ⅛ inch from the stitched lines and directly on the top and bottom (curved) lines. Turn the cuff right side out. Set aside.

Place the heel and toe on the stocking front, and stitch them in place along the inside edges. With the right sides facing, sew the stocking pieces together, leaving the top edge unstitched. Trim the seam allowance, and then turn the stocking right side out and press.

Pin the cuff inside the stocking, matching the straight edges. *Note:* The right side of the cuff will face the wrong side of the stocking. Stitch around the top edge using a ½-inch seam allowance. Turn the cuff right side out. Tack a large bell to each point. Sew smaller bells to the toe and heel, stitching the bell loops to the back of the stocking.

Using spray adhesive, add a scrap Santa motif to the front. Fold the hanging loop strip in half. Neatly hand-sew the short edges together with whipstitches. Sew the whipstitched edge at the seam line inside the cuff.

Photograph by Marty Baldwin

Santa is sure to leave a prize or two in a vintage-style stocking made of old-fashioned cotton batting and paper scrap.

ICICLE-TRIMMED STOCKING

With a pencil, trace the outline of the stocking pattern *opposite* onto tracing paper. Enlarge pattern 200 percent, and cut it out.

Cut two 12x20-inch rectangles from the cotton batting. Press out any wrinkles. Place the rectangles with matching sides facing. Trace the outline of the stocking shape onto the top rectangle using the marking pen.

Stitch around the stocking, leaving the top edge unstitched. Using the straight-edge scissors, cut out the stocking ⅛ inch from the stitching line, and cut straight across the top. Turn the stocking right side out and press.

Place the wrong side of the icicle border facing the right side of the stocking. Wrap the icicle border around the top of the stocking, keeping the straight edges even and overlapping the border in the center back. Sew the border in place ¼ inch from the top edge.

Using silver metallic thread and an embroidery needle, hand-sew the tinsel garland around the top of the stocking, forming a hanging loop at one side.

Adhere the scrap Santa motif to the stocking front with spray adhesive.

PINKED-EDGE STOCKING

With a pencil, trace the stocking pattern *opposite* onto tracing paper. Enlarge pattern 200 percent; cut it out.

From the cotton batting, cut two 12x20-inch rectangles. Press out any

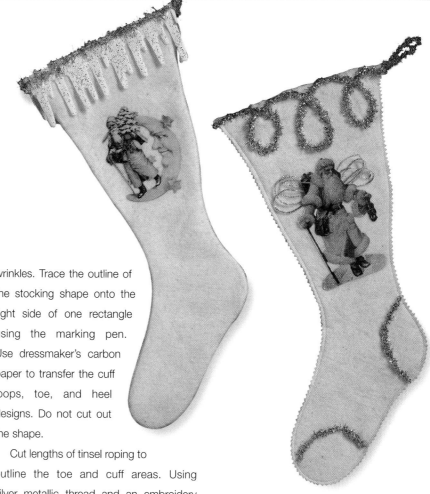

wrinkles. Trace the outline of the stocking shape onto the right side of one rectangle using the marking pen. Use dressmaker's carbon paper to transfer the cuff loops, toe, and heel designs. Do not cut out the shape.

Cut lengths of tinsel roping to outline the toe and cuff areas. Using silver metallic thread and an embroidery needle, hand-sew the roping to the stocking front, keeping the roping away from the outline.

Place the batting rectangles together with the wrong sides facing. Stitch around the stocking, leaving the top edge unstitched. Cut out the stocking ¼ inch from the stitching line using pinking shears. Use the straight-edge scissors to cut across the top. Do not turn the stocking right side out.

Decorate the stocking cuff with the remaining roping as follows: Starting in the center back and working toward the toe, pin the roping along the top edge. Turn the corner, and then create the loops across the front.

Form a small hanging loop at the heel side, and then turn the corner and pin the remaining roping even with the top edge of the stocking back. Cut away any excess roping. Hand-sew the roping in place with metallic thread.

Wrap crinkle wire around the cardboard, creating four loops at each end. Gently remove the wire. Pinch the loops in the center, and wrap that spot with a short length of wire. Tack the center of the loops to the stocking front 5 inches below the center top. Using spray adhesive, adhere the scrap Santa motif to the stocking front over the wire loops. Referring to the photo *above,* gently stretch the loops. ✦

Designed by Laura Collins

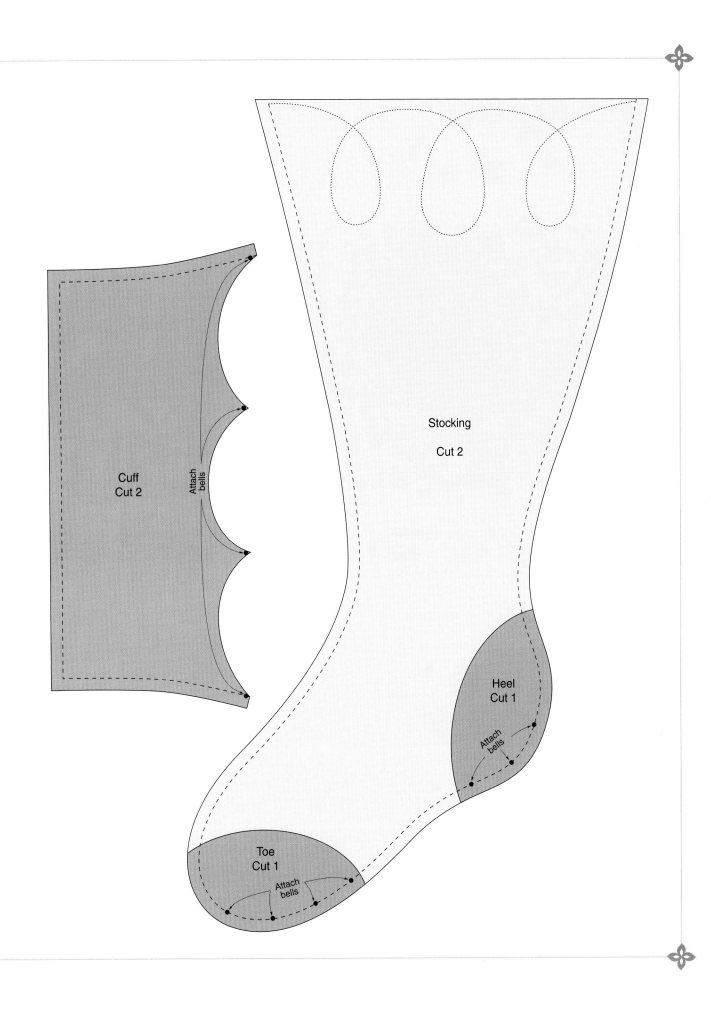

Cuff
Cut 2

Attach
bells

Stocking

Cut 2

Heel
Cut 1

Attach
bells

Toe
Cut 1

Attach
bells

Candy-Cane Santa

Photograph by Marty Balduin

The Santa is 20 inches tall.

MATERIALS

For all stockings:

- **Tracing paper**
- **½ cup instant coffee**
- **⅓ yard of Osnaburg fabric**
- **Rubber gloves**
- **¼ yard of red wool felt**
- **⅛ yard of white wool felt**
- **¼ yard of red striped fabric**
- **⅛ yard of black cotton fabric**
- **Pinking shears**
- **Matching sewing threads**
- **Polyester fiberfill**
- **Long needle**
- **Acrylic paints: blue, brown, red iron oxide, and white**
- **Paintbrush**
- **Brown fine-tip permanent marker**
- **Powder blush**
- **Silver quilting pencil**
- **Heavy string**
- **Tapestry needle**
- **Glue gun and hotmelt adhesive**
- **Sheep wool fleece**
- **Three each of red and cream chenille sticks**
- **Wire cutters**

GENERAL DIRECTIONS

Trace the patterns on *pages 140–143* onto tracing paper. Cut out the pattern pieces. Sew all pieces with right sides together, using ¼-inch seam allowances unless otherwise noted. The pattern outlines for the body, arm, and boot are sewing lines. The pattern outlines for the coat, hat, and star are cutting lines.

PREPARE THE FABRIC

Bring one quart of water to a boil. Remove from heat and mix instant coffee with the water. Immerse the Osnaburg fabric in the mixture. Let stand for ten minutes. Wearing rubber gloves, squeeze the water out of the fabric and hang to dry. Press to remove the wrinkles.

CUT THE FABRICS

From the red wool felt, cut two coats, one hat, and three stars. From the white wool felt, cut one 1¼x10½-inch strip for the coat trim, two ¾x2¾-inch strips for the sleeve trim, three 1¼-inch diameter circles, one 1x5½-inch strip for the hatband, and one ½x14-inch strip for the hat stripe. Referring to the photograph *opposite,* cut ¾-inch-tall triangles from one long edge of the coat trim using the pinking shears. Also use the

pinking shears to trim both long edges of the hat stripe, one long edge of each sleeve trim, and the edges of the circles.

From the striped fabric, cut two 5x9-inch rectangles for the pants with the stripes running lengthwise.

MAKE THE BODY

Fold the Osnaburg fabric in half with the right sides together. With a pencil, trace around the body pattern once on one side of the doubled fabric. Sew the layers together, stitching on the traced lines and leaving the bottom edge open. Cut out the body, leaving a ¼-inch seam allowance. Clip the curves, turn the body right side out, and press.

Firmly stuff the body with polyester fiberfill. Turn under the raw edges at the opening; slip-stitch the opening closed. Use a pencil to lightly draw a U on the center of the face a scant ¼ inch wide and ⅞ inch tall. Thread a long needle with thread to match the fabric; knot the ends together. Insert the needle at the seam at the top of the head and come up at the top left of the U. Insert the needle ⅛ inch below the top left corner of the U and come up at the top right corner, catching a small amount of stuffing as you run the needle

This folk-art fellow, holding an armload of chenille candy canes and a bottle-brush tree, is decked out in his holiday best for greeting guests.

under the fabric. Pull the thread snugly to raise the nose area. Next, insert the needle ⅛ inch below the top right corner of the U and come up on the left side at the last stitch. Continue in this manner down the vertical lines of the U, dipping into the fiber-fill with each stitch and pulling the thread tightly. For the bottom of the nose, insert the needle at the center bottom of the U and come up at the last stitch on the right; pull the thread tight. Insert the needle into the side of the nose and come up at the top of the head. Tie and cut the thread.

Referring to the photograph on *page 139* and the pattern on *page 142,* use a pencil to very lightly draw the eyes on the face. Paint white eyes and eyebrows; let dry. Paint the irises blue; dot brown centers on the eyes. When the paint is dry, add a tiny white highlight dot to each eye. Use red iron oxide to paint a tiny mouth line. Outline each eye with a brown fine-tip permanent marker. Color cheeks with powdered blush.

Fold the black fabric in half with right sides facing. With a silver quilting pencil, trace around the arm twice and the boot twice on one side of the black fabric, leaving at least ½ inch between the shapes. Sew the layers together, stitching on the traced lines and leaving the edges open as indicated on the patterns. Cut the arms and boots out, leaving a ¼-inch seam allowance. Clip the curves, turn the pieces right side out, and press. Firmly stuff the arms and boots with fiberfill.

SEW THE CLOTHING

Coat: Sew the coat front to the back at the shoulder seams, leaving a neck opening as

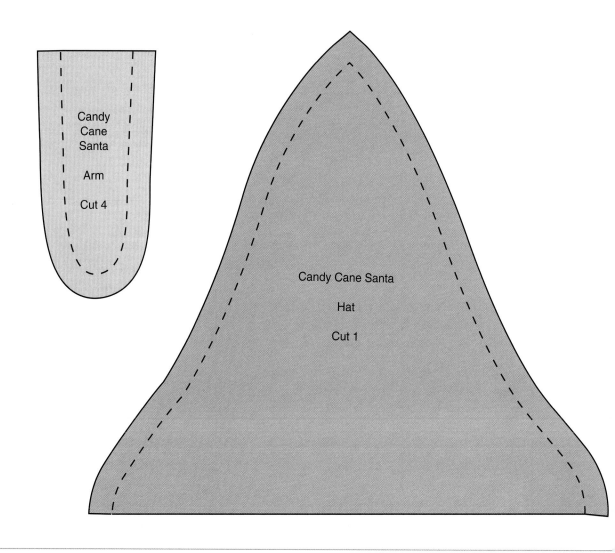

Candy Cane Santa

Arm

Cut 4

Candy Cane Santa

Hat

Cut 1

indicated on the pattern. Place a sleeve trim on the wrong side of each sleeve so ¼ inch of the trim extends beyond the bottom edge of the sleeve; edgestitch in place. Sew the coat front to the back at one underarm/side seam. Place the coat trim on the wrong side of the coat so the pinked edge extends beyond the bottom edge of the coat; edgestitch in place. Sew the remaining underarm/side seam. Clip the inside corners; turn the coat right side out.

Use straight stitches and red thread to sew a star on each white felt circle. Position the circles on the center front of the coat, beginning ¼ inch from the coat's bottom edge and leaving ¼ inch between the circles. Straight-stitch the circles to the coat with white thread.

Pants: Sew together the two 5x9-inch rectangles of striped fabric along the 9-inch edges. Find the center of one 5-inch edge, and use a pencil to draw a line extending

5 inches into the fabric for the inseam. Sew ¼ inch around the drawn inseam line; cut on the line. Turn the pants right side out.

To create casings, press under ½ inch at the waist and the bottoms of the pant legs; sew ¼ inch from the pressed edges. For the waist, carefully cut through the front layer only of the casing at the center front. Thread a tapestry needle with heavy string and work it through the casing, beginning and ending at the center front. For the leg casings, cut through the outside layer only of the casing at the inseam. Thread heavy string through each pant leg, beginning and ending at the inseam.

Hat: Fold the hatband in half, aligning the long edges. Place the hatband along the bottom edge of the hat so the folded edge of the band extends ¼ inch beyond the bottom edge of the hat; edgestitch in place. Fold the hat in half and sew together the center back edges. Trim any excess

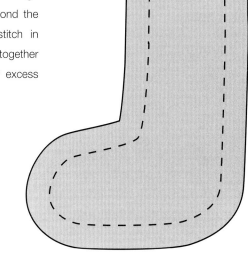

Candy
Cane
Santa

Leg

Cut 4

Candy Cane
Santa

Cut 3

Candy Cane
Santa

Cut 3

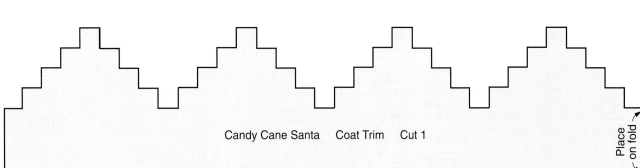

Candy Cane Santa   Coat Trim   Cut 1

Place
on fold

bulk. Turn the hat right side out. Wrap the pinked hat stripe around the hat to resemble a candy cane; pin in place. Use running stitches and white thread to sew the stripe to the hat.

FINISH THE SANTA

To attach the boots, slip a boot into each pant leg. Pull the strings to gather the pant legs snugly around the boots, adjusting the gathers evenly. Double-knot to secure, and trim the excess string to 1 inch. Tuck the string ends into the pant legs. Adjust the height of the boots in the pant legs so 2 inches of boot extend beyond the bottom edge of each pant leg. Tack the pant legs to the boots to secure.

Slip the pants on the doll. Pull the string to fit the pants snugly around the waist, and knot to secure; trim the excess string.

Hot-glue or tack an arm into each sleeve so the hand extends 1 inch beyond the sleeve trim. Lightly stuff the sleeves with fiberfill. Slip the coat onto the doll.

For the beard, gently pull the fleece into sections long enough for the beard. Apply hot glue in a semicircle to frame the bottom of the face about $\frac{1}{4}$ inch below the mouth. Pinching the fleece between your fingertips, apply sections to cover the glue. Apply additional layers of fleece as needed to create a full beard.

For the mustache, select a curly 2-inch piece of fleece. Moisten your fingertips, and twist each end to a point. Knot one end of a thread length around the center of the mustache. Thread the opposite end into a needle. Insert the needle into the face between the nose and the mouth.

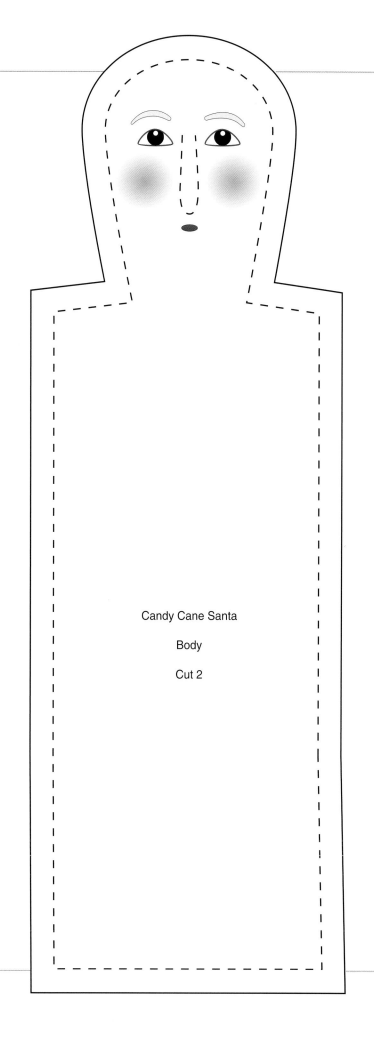

Candy Cane Santa

Body

Cut 2

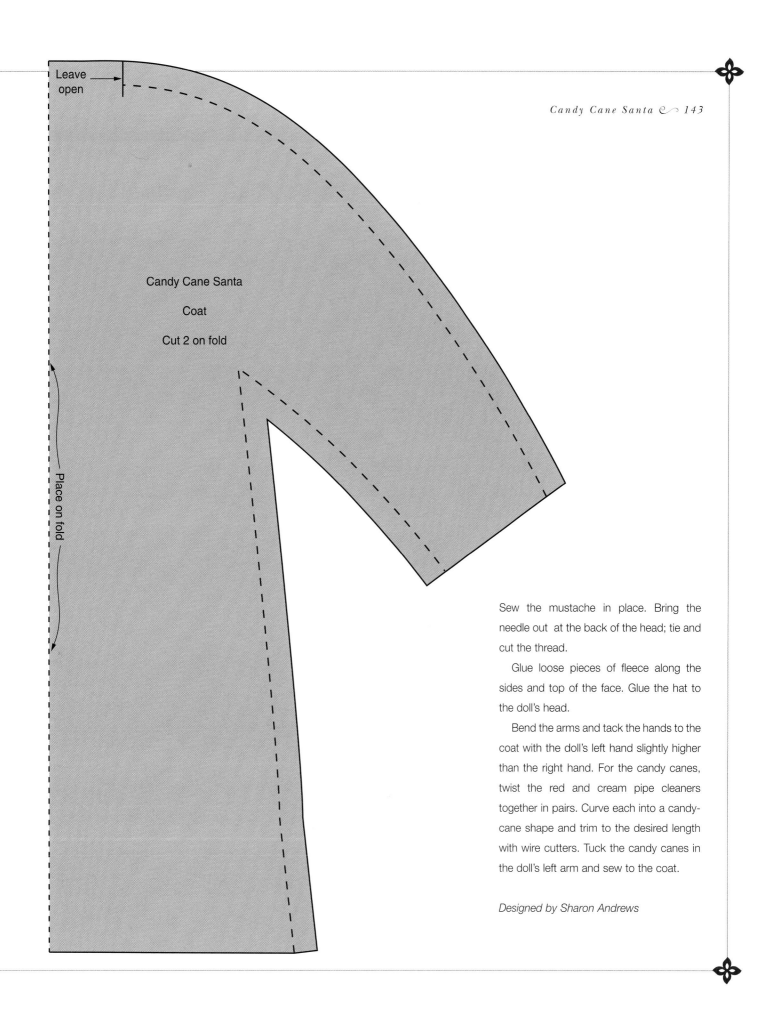

Leave open

Candy Cane Santa

Coat

Cut 2 on fold

Place on fold

Sew the mustache in place. Bring the needle out at the back of the head; tie and cut the thread.

Glue loose pieces of fleece along the sides and top of the face. Glue the hat to the doll's head.

Bend the arms and tack the hands to the coat with the doll's left hand slightly higher than the right hand. For the candy canes, twist the red and cream pipe cleaners together in pairs. Curve each into a candy-cane shape and trim to the desired length with wire cutters. Tuck the candy canes in the doll's left arm and sew to the coat.

Designed by Sharon Andrews

SWEET SENSATIONS

Santa will drop in for a

prolonged stop at your house

on Christmas Eve when you

entice him with a plateful of

delectable cookies. Save a few

of your treats for other visitors,

too, and cozy up for a long

chat over a batch of cookies

and a hot mug of cocoa.

*A plateful of cookies is the perfect
treat for any holiday occasion.*

Photograph by Scott Little

Cookies for Santa

CHOOSE COOKIES FROM THIS FESTIVE SAMPLER TO ADD EVEN
GREATER JOY TO YOUR FAMILY'S HOLIDAY CELEBRATION.

ROLY-POLY SANTAS

When shaping the cookies, press the balls of dough against each other as you flatten them so they won't separate after baking.

Prep: 1 hr. Bake: 12 min. per batch

1	cup butter, softened
½	cup sugar
1	tablespoon milk
1	teaspoon vanilla
2¼	cups all-purpose flour
	Red paste food coloring
	Miniature semisweet chocolate pieces
	Snow Frosting (recipe, page 151)
	Red cinnamon candies

Preheat oven to 325°F. In a large mixing bowl beat butter with an electric mixer on medium to high speed for 30 seconds. Add sugar; beat until combined, scraping sides of bowl occasionally. Beat in milk and vanilla. Beat in as much of the flour as you can with the mixer. Stir in any remaining flour with a wooden spoon. Remove 1 cup of dough. Stir red paste food coloring into remaining dough to make desired color.

Shape each Santa by making one ¾-inch ball and five ¼-inch balls from plain dough. From red dough, shape one 1-inch ball and five ½-inch balls. Flatten the 1-inch red ball on an ungreased cookie sheet until ½ inch thick. Attach the ¾-inch plain ball for head and flatten until ½ inch thick. Attach

four ½-inch red balls for arms and legs. Shape remaining ½-inch red ball into a hat. Place plain ¼-inch balls at ends of arms and legs for hands and feet and at the tip of the hat. Add chocolate pieces for eyes and buttons.

Bake in preheated oven for 12 to 15 minutes or until edges are light brown. Cool on cookie sheet for 2 minutes. Transfer cookies to wire racks and cool completely.

Spoon Snow Frosting into a decorating bag fitted with a medium star tip. Pipe frosting for mustache, beard, and hatband. For nose, attach a cinnamon candy with a small dab of frosting. Let frosting dry. *Makes 12.*

Written by Janet Figg ◆ *Food styling by Jennifer Peterson* ◆ *Photographs by Pete Krumhardt and Scott Little*

Clockwise from far left:
Roly-Poly Santas (recipe
opposite), Star Santas,
and Half-Moon Santas
(recipe, page 148)

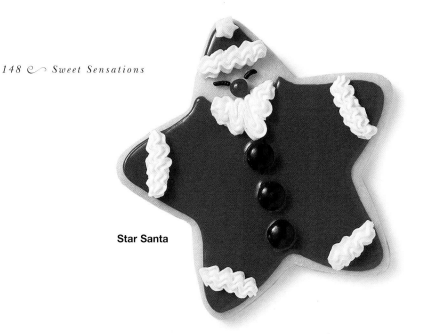

Star Santa

SANTA CUTOUTS

Use this recipe to create Star Santas, Diamond Santas, Triangle Santas, and Half-Moon Santas.

Prep: 50 min. Chill: 3 hrs.
Bake: 7 min. per batch

⅓ cup butter, softened
⅓ cup shortening
¾ cup granulated sugar
1 teaspoon baking powder
 Dash salt
1 egg
1 tablespoon milk
1 teaspoon vanilla
2 cups all-purpose flour
 Egg Paint (recipe, page 151)
 Snow Frosting (recipe, page 151)
 Powdered Sugar Icing (recipe, page 151)
 Assorted toppers and candies, such as clear and red edible glitter, plain and colored sanding sugar, miniature semisweet chocolate pieces, and candy-coated chocolate pieces

In a large mixing bowl beat butter and shortening with an electric mixer on medium to high speed for 30 seconds. Add granulated sugar, baking powder, and salt; beat until combined. Beat in egg, milk,

and vanilla. Beat in as much of the flour you can with the mixer. Stir in any remaining flour with a wooden spoon. Cover dough; refrigerate about 3 hours or until dough is easy to handle.

Preheat oven to 375°F. On a lightly floured surface roll dough until ⅛ inch thick. Cut into desired shapes (see instructions below and at right). Place shapes 1 inch apart on an ungreased cookie sheet. Paint with Egg Paint, as desired, according to instructions.

Bake in preheated oven for 7 to 8 minutes or until the bottoms are light brown. Cool on cookie sheet for 1 minute. Transfer cookies to wire racks; cool. Decorate as desired with Snow Frosting, Powdered Sugar Icing, and/or candies. Let icing or frosting dry.

Star Santas: Cut dough into stars with a 4-inch cookie cutter. Paint coats and hats with red-tinted Egg Paint before baking. Pipe Snow Frosting for textured areas and Powdered Sugar Icing for fine details. Attach candies for buttons, eyes, and noses with small dabs of frosting. *Makes 36.*

Diamond Santas: Cut dough into diamonds with a 2½- to 3½-inch cookie cutter. For smooth, red caps, brush Egg Paint on cap areas before baking. For more textured caps, spoon red-tinted Snow Frosting into a decorating bag fitted with a medium star tip; pipe frosting in cap area and for hatband and mustache. For fine details, spoon Powdered Sugar Icing into a decorating bag fitted with a writing tip; pipe where desired. *Makes 40.*

Triangle Santas: Cut dough into triangles with a 3-inch cookie cutter. Paint coat area with red-tinted Egg Paint before baking. Pipe Snow Frosting where a textured look is desired; pipe Powdered Sugar Icing for fine details. *Makes 40.*

Half-Moon Santas: Cut dough into half-moon shapes with a 2½-inch cookie cutter. Paint caps with Egg Paint before baking. Pipe beard with Powdered Sugar Icing; sprinkle with sugar. Attach candy for eyes and noses with frosting. *Makes 45.*

Madeleine Santa (recipe, page 152)

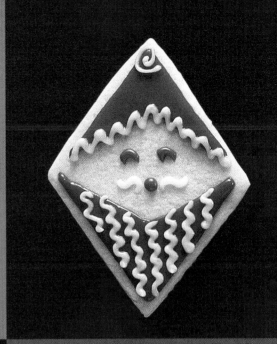

Jolly St. Nicks

MADELEINE SANTAS
The plump, rounded shape of
these cookies provides a head start
toward whimsical results.

TRIANGLE SANTAS
For fun, use a zigzag-edge cutter.
Decorate cutouts to face
forward or in profile.

DIAMOND SANTAS
This shape is made to order for
fashioning peaked red hats and
pointed white beards.

Front: Santa's Whiskers
Back: Apple Butter Bars

APPLE BUTTER BARS

Apple butter adds pleasing spiciness and fruit flavor to these moist bars.
Prep: 20 min. Bake: 25 min.

1	6-ounce package (1½ cups) mixed dried fruit
½	cup butter, softened
¾	cup packed brown sugar
½	teaspoon baking soda
½	teaspoon ground cinnamon
¼	teaspoon salt
2	eggs
½	cup apple butter
1½	cups all-purpose flour
	Powdered sugar

Preheat oven to 350°F. Pour boiling water over fruit bits to cover. Let stand for 5 minutes; drain.

Meanwhile, in a large mixing bowl beat butter with an electric mixer on medium to high speed for 30 seconds. Add brown sugar, baking soda, cinnamon, and salt; beat until combined, scraping sides of bowl occasionally. Beat in eggs and apple butter until combined. Beat in as much of the flour as you can with the mixer. Stir in any remaining flour and the drained fruit with a wooden spoon.

Spread batter in a greased 13x9x2-inch baking pan. Bake in preheated oven for 25 to 30 minutes or until done. Cool in pan on a wire rack. Sift powdered sugar over top; cut into bars. *Makes 36.*

SANTA'S WHISKERS

The shaggy coconut that clings to each cookie slice represents St. Nick's beard.
Prep: 30 min. Chill: 2 hrs.
Bake: 8 min. per batch

¾	cup butter, softened
¾	cup sugar
1	tablespoon milk
1	teaspoon vanilla
2	cups all-purpose flour
¾	cup finely chopped candied red and/or green cherries
⅓	cup finely chopped pecans
¾	cup shredded coconut

In a large mixing bowl beat butter with an electric mixer on medium to high speed for 30 seconds. Add sugar and beat until combined, scraping sides of bowl occasionally. Beat in milk and vanilla until combined. Beat in as much of the flour as you can with the mixer. Stir in any remaining flour, the candied cherries, and the pecans with a wooden spoon.

Divide dough in half; shape each half into an 8-inch-long loaf. Roll each loaf in coconut. Wrap each loaf in plastic wrap or waxed paper and refrigerate for 2 to 24 hours.

Preheat oven to 375°F. Cut loaves into ¼-inch-thick slices. Place slices 1 inch apart on an ungreased cookie sheet. Bake for 8 to 10 minutes or until edges are golden brown. Transfer cookies to wire racks and cool. *Makes about 60.*

SANTA DECORATING RECIPES

Egg Paint

In a small bowl stir together 1 *egg yolk* and 2 drops *water.* Stir in *paste food coloring* to make paint of desired color. Apply paint to cookies before baking so the egg mixture cooks fully.

Snow Frosting

In a small bowl beat ½ cup *shortening* and ½ teaspoon *vanilla* with an electric mixer on medium speed for 30 seconds. Gradually beat in 1⅓ cups sifted *powdered sugar.* Add 1 tablespoon *milk.* Gradually beat in 1 cup sifted *powdered sugar* and enough milk (3 to 4 teaspoons) to make a frosting of piping consistency. Color the frosting as desired with *paste food coloring.* Use a decorating bag and star tip to pipe frosting in areas where texture is desired.

Powdered Sugar Icing

In a small bowl stir together 4 cups sifted *powdered sugar,* 1 teaspoon *vanilla,* and enough *milk* (about 3 to 4 tablespoons) to make an icing of piping consistency. Color icing as desired with *paste food coloring.* Use a decorating bag and writing tip to pipe fine details.

OLD-FASHIONED SUGAR COOKIES

To sour milk for these big, soft cookies, combine 1 tablespoon lemon juice or vinegar and enough milk to make 1 cup; let stand for 5 minutes.

Prep: 20 min. Chill: 3 hrs.
Bake: 10 min. per batch

1¼   cups shortening
2   cups granulated sugar
2   teaspoons baking powder
1   teaspoon baking soda
½   teaspoon ground nutmeg
¼   teaspoon salt
2   eggs
1   teaspoon vanilla
½   teaspoon lemon extract
4½   cups all-purpose flour
1   cup buttermilk or sour milk
   Coarse colored sugar, fine sanding sugar, or granulated sugar

In a large mixing bowl, beat shortening with an electric mixer on medium to high speed for 30 seconds. Add the 2 cups sugar, baking powder, baking soda, nutmeg, and salt; beat until combined, scraping sides of bowl occasionally. Beat in eggs, vanilla, and lemon extract until combined. Alternately add flour and buttermilk to shortening mixture, beating until combined. Divide dough in half. Cover dough and refrigerate at least 3 hours or until easy to handle.

Preheat oven to 375°F. On a floured surface roll dough until ½ inch thick. Cut dough into rounds with a 2½-inch cookie cutter. Place rounds 2½ inches apart on an ungreased cookie sheet. Sprinkle with additional sugar. Bake in preheated oven about 10 minutes or until set and edges just begin to brown. Transfer cookies to wire racks and cool. *Makes 32.*

MADELEINE SANTAS

Transform shell-shape madeleine cookies into an assortment of splendid Santas with beards of snowy white frosting. Pictured on page 148.

Prep: 1¼ hrs. Bake: 10 min. per batch

2   eggs
½   teaspoon vanilla
½   teaspoon finely shredded lemon peel
1   cup sifted powdered sugar
⅔   cup all-purpose flour
¼   teaspoon baking powder
½   cup butter, melted and cooled
   Snow Frosting (recipe, page 151)
   Powdered Sugar Icing (recipe, page 151)
   Assorted decorative candies
   Powdered sugar

Preheat oven to 375°F. Grease and flour twenty-four 3-inch madeleine pan molds*; set aside.

In a medium mixing bowl beat eggs, vanilla, and lemon peel with an electric mixer on high speed for 5 minutes. Gradually beat in the 1 cup powdered sugar. Beat for 5 to 7 minutes or until batter is thick and satiny.

Sift together flour and baking powder. Sift one-fourth of flour mixture over egg mixture; gently stir. Stir in remaining flour one-fourth at a time. Stir in butter.

Spoon batter into prepared molds, filling each mold three-fourths full.

Bake in preheated oven for 10 to 12 minutes or until edges are golden and tops spring back when lightly pressed. Cool in molds on wire racks for 1 minute. Loosen cookies with a knife. Invert onto wire racks and cool.

Decorate cookies, as desired, using Snow Frosting, Powdered Sugar Icing, candies, and powdered sugar. For a textured look, pipe Snow Frosting from a decorating bag fitted with a medium star tip. To add fine details, pipe Powdered Sugar Icing from a decorating bag fitted with a writing tip. Allow icing or frosting to dry. *Makes 24.*

* To order a madeleine pan, see Sources, page 159.

COOKIE STORAGE TIPS

To store baked cookies, follow these guidelines:
• Make sure the cookies have cooled completely before storing. If they are still warm, they're likely to stick together.
• Use plastic bags or containers with airtight lids for storage.
• Store crisp and soft cookies separately.
• Plan on keeping cookies at room temperature for up to 1 week or freeze for up to 3 months.
• Store cookies unfrosted. Frosting may cause cookies to stick together. Thaw cookies, then decorate.

Old-Fashioned Sugar Cookies

Front: Date Pinwheel Cookies
Back: Date and Orange Pockets and
Sour Cream and Chocolate Drops
(recipe, page 156)

DATE PINWHEEL COOKIES

For uniform slices, cut the well-chilled dough rolls with a thin, sharp knife, using a sawing motion.

Prep: 40 min. Chill: 1 + 2 to 24 hrs.
Bake: 8 min. per batch

- 1 8-ounce package (1⅓ cups) pitted whole dates, finely snipped
- ½ cup water
- ⅓ cup granulated sugar
- 2 tablespoons lemon juice
- ½ teaspoon vanilla
- ½ cup shortening
- ½ cup butter, softened
- ½ cup granulated sugar
- ½ cup packed brown sugar
- ½ teaspoon baking soda
- ¼ teaspoon salt
- 1 egg
- 3 tablespoons milk
- 1 teaspoon vanilla
- 3 cups all-purpose flour

For filling, in a saucepan combine dates, water, and the ⅓ cup granulated sugar. Bring to boiling; reduce heat. Cook and stir for 2 minutes or until thick. Stir in lemon juice and the ½ teaspoon vanilla; cool.

In a large mixing bowl beat shortening and butter with an electric mixer on medium to high speed for 30 seconds. Add the ½ cup granulated sugar, brown sugar, baking soda, and salt. Beat until combined, scraping sides of bowl occasionally.

Beat in egg, milk, and the 1 teaspoon vanilla. Beat in as much of the flour as you can with the mixer. Stir in remaining flour with a wooden spoon. Divide dough in half. Cover dough and refrigerate for 1 hour or until easy to handle.

Place half of the dough between two pieces of waxed paper. Roll dough into a 12×10-inch rectangle. Spread with half of the filling. Beginning with a long edge, carefully roll up the dough and filling. Moisten edges; pinch to seal. Wrap dough roll in plastic wrap or waxed paper. Repeat with remaining dough and filling. Chill rolls for 2 to 24 hours or until firm enough to slice.

Preheat oven to 375°F. Cut rolls into ¼-inch-thick slices. Place slices 1 inch apart on a greased cookie sheet. Bake for 8 to 10 minutes or until edges are light brown. Transfer cookies to wire racks and cool. *Makes 64.*

DATE AND ORANGE POCKETS

Wait until you bite into one of these filled cookies! They're stuffed with dates and nuts.

Prep: 25 min. Chill: 1 hr.
Bake: 7 min. per batch

- ½ cup butter, softened
- ⅔ cup packed brown sugar
- 1 teaspoon baking powder
- ½ teaspoon ground cinnamon
- ⅛ teaspoon salt
- 1 egg
- ½ teaspoon vanilla
- 1 cup all-purpose flour
- ⅔ cup whole wheat flour
- 1 8-ounce package sugar-coated chopped pitted dates
- ⅓ cup orange juice
- ¼ cup granulated sugar
- ¼ cup chopped walnuts or pecans
  Golden Icing

In a large mixing bowl beat butter with an electric mixer on medium to high speed for 30 seconds. Add brown sugar, baking powder, cinnamon, and salt. Beat until combined, scraping sides of bowl occasionally. Beat in egg and vanilla until combined. Beat or stir in flours. Cover dough and refrigerate about 1 hour or until firm enough to handle.

Meanwhile, for filling, in a food processor or blender combine dates, orange juice, granulated sugar, and nuts. Cover and process or blend until smooth, stopping to scrape sides.

Preheat oven to 375°F. On a lightly floured surface roll dough until ⅛ inch thick. Cut dough into rounds with a 2½-inch cookie cutter. Place rounds ½ inch apart on an ungreased cookie sheet. Spoon 1 level teaspoon of the date filling into center of each round. Fold round in half over filling, forming a half-moon shape. Seal edges with the tines of a fork.

Bake for 7 to 9 minutes or until edges are firm and bottoms are light brown. Transfer cookies to wire racks and cool. Drizzle with Golden Icing. *Makes about 48.*

Golden Icing: In a saucepan heat 2 tablespoons *butter* over medium-low heat for 10 to 12 minutes or until light brown. Remove from heat. Gradually stir in ¾ cup sifted *powdered sugar* and ¼ teaspoon *vanilla* (mixture will be crumbly). Gradually stir in enough *milk* (2 to 3 teaspoons) to make an icing of drizzling consistency.

SOUR CREAM AND CHOCOLATE DROPS

Got a chocolate lover on your gift list? Surprise that person with a box of these chocolate delights, made extra fudgy with Chocolate Butter Frosting. Pictured on page 154.

Prep: 30 min. Bake: 8 min. per batch

½	cup butter, softened
1	cup packed brown sugar
½	teaspoon baking soda
¼	teaspoon salt
1	8-ounce carton dairy sour cream
2	ounces unsweetened chocolate, melted and cooled
1	egg
1	teaspoon vanilla
2	cups all-purpose flour
	Chocolate Butter Frosting

Preheat oven to 350°F. In a large mixing bowl beat butter with an electric mixer on medium to high speed for 30 seconds. Add brown sugar, baking soda, and salt. Beat until combined, scraping sides of bowl occasionally. Beat in sour cream, chocolate, egg, and vanilla until combined. Beat in as much of the flour as you can with the mixer. Stir in any remaining flour with a wooden spoon.

Drop dough by slightly rounded teaspoons 2 inches apart onto an ungreased cookie sheet. Bake in preheated oven for 8 to 10 minutes or until edges are firm. Transfer cookies to wire racks; cool. Spread cooled cookies with Chocolate Butter Frosting. *Makes about 42.*

Chocolate Butter Frosting: In a medium mixing bowl beat ¼ cup softened *butter* for 30 seconds. Gradually add 1 cup sifted *powdered sugar* and ⅓ cup *unsweetened cocoa powder*, beating well. Slowly beat in 3 tablespoons *milk* and 1 teaspoon *vanilla*. Slowly beat in an additional 1½ cups sifted *powdered sugar*. If necessary, beat in additional milk to make a frosting of spreading consistency.

SPICY GINGER HEARTS

Two surprise ingredients—black pepper and grated fresh ginger—lend spiciness to these heartwarming cutouts.

Prep: 40 min. Chill: 4 hrs.

Bake: 10 min. per batch

¾	cup butter, softened
¾	cup packed brown sugar
2	tablespoons grated fresh ginger or 2 teaspoons ground ginger
1½	teaspoons finely ground black pepper
½	teaspoon baking soda
¼	teaspoon salt
¼	teaspoon ground cinnamon
¼	teaspoon ground nutmeg
1	egg
⅓	cup molasses
2¾	cups all-purpose flour
	Royal Icing or purchased decorator icing
	Red and white nonpareils or other small red candies (optional)

In a large mixing bowl beat butter with an electric mixer on medium to high speed for 30 seconds. Add brown sugar, ginger, pepper, baking soda, salt, cinnamon, and nutmeg. Beat until combined, scraping sides of bowl occasionally. Beat in egg and molasses until combined. Beat in as much of the flour as you can with the mixer. Stir in remaining flour with a wooden spoon.

Divide the dough in half. Cover and refrigerate for 4 to 24 hours or until dough is easy to handle.

Preheat oven to 350°F. Lightly grease cookie sheets or line with parchment paper; set aside.

On a lightly floured surface roll half of the dough at a time until ¼ inch thick. Cut dough using heart-shape cookie cutters of various sizes. Place cutouts about 1 inch apart on prepared cookie sheet. If you plan to hang the cookie, use a drinking straw to make a hole at the top of the cookie before baking.

Bake in preheated oven about 10 minutes or until tops of cookies appear dry. Cool on cookie sheet for 1 minute. Transfer cookies to wire racks and cool. Decorate cooled cookies, as desired, with Royal Icing and nonpareils or other candies. *Makes about 24.*

Royal Icing: In a medium mixing bowl combine 2 cups sifted *powdered sugar* and 4 teaspoons *meringue powder*. Add 3 tablespoons *cold water*. Beat with an electric mixer on low speed until combined; beat on medium to high speed for 5 to 8 minutes or until very stiff peaks form. (If mixture seems stiff while beating, add water, ½ teaspoon at a time, until icing is of desired consistency. Icing should be fairly thick for piping.) If desired, transfer some icing to another bowl and color with red *paste food coloring*. When not using icing, keep it tightly covered to prevent it from drying out; keep refrigerated.

Spicy Ginger Hearts

Sources

Timeless Memorabilia

Gold Horse Publishing, Inc., *pages 26–31*
P.O. Box 151, Annapolis, MD 21404
800/966-3655
Theriault's the Dollmasters Web site:
www.theriaults.com

Twins Feather Trees, Inc., *pages 32–37*
1543 Pullan Ave., Cincinnati, OH 45223
513/681-9357
www.twinsfeathertrees.com
E-mail: twinsfeathertree@mindspring.com

Inge-*glas* USA, LLC, *pages 38–45*
P.O. Box 1748, Ashland, VA 23005
888/596-5910 or 804/798-1980
www.inge-glas.com

White feather tree as seen in inge-glas story:
The Feather Tree Company, *pages 43–44*
P.O. Box 281, Sun Prairie, WI 53590
608/837-7669
www.feathertrees.com

Devoted Collectors

Golden Glow of Christmas
Winsdale St., Golden Valley, MN 55427-4250
http://my.execpc.com/~gmoe/gg-web2

Debbee Thibault, *pages 58–61*
Call 562/402-6171 for general information and a list of stores in your area (Debbee Thibault's American Collectibles sells wholesale to stores only, and no retail to collectors).
www.debbeethibault.com
E-mail: debbeethibault.Ac@verizon.net

Master Crafters

Carving Out His Niche, *pages 70–75*
The Whimsical Whittler
1745 West Columbia Rd., Mason, MI 48854
517/676-4846
www.whimsicalwhittler.com
E-mail: whimsicalwhit@aol.com
For catalogue, send $3.00 and SASE.

Simply Vintage, *pages 76–81*
Nicol Sayre Folk Dolls
P.O. Box 11394, Pleasanton, CA 94588
www.nicolsayre.com
E-mail: nicol@nicolsayre.com

Tea-color feather tree as seen in Nicol Sayre story:
Tannenbaum Shop, *page 79*
Northville, Michigan
248/349-3423
E-mail: thetannenbaumshop@yahoo.com

Wood case as seen in Nicol Sayre story:
James Main, *pages 80*
21 Tinkham Rd.
North Bennington, VT 05257
802/440-9688

For Goodness' Sake, *pages 82–87*
Sharon Andrews and Company
www.sharonandrewsandcompany.com

In Search of the Perfect Santa, *pages 88–93*
Lois Clarkson Snowdin Studios
P.O. Box 28, Buckingham, PA 18912
E-mail: Snowdinstudios@aol.com
Photos available by request

A Collector's Passion, *pages 94–99*
Paul Gordon
204 South Queen Street, Martinsburg, WV 25401
304/260-0020
For brochure please enclose a check for $4.

Whimsical Wonders, *pages 100–105*
Snickles and Kringles
123 Chestnut St., Haddonfield, NJ 08033
856/354-8224

Born-Again Belsnickles, *pages 106-111*
Nyla Murphy
219 Union St., Milford, MI 48381-1968
E-mail: nylamurph@aol.com
For brochure please enclose a check for $3.

Telling Tales, *pages 112–117*
Susan McMullen
E-mail: mcmullens@mackbc.com
For questions regarding Santas, contact exclusive sales agent Alisa Benaresh at 732/864-0466.

The Art of Santa, *pages 118–125*
Jack Johnston Studios
Johnston Academy of Art Dolls
530 Tanglewood Loop
North Salt Lake City, UT 84054
800/290-9998
www.artdolls.com
How-to educational videos, books, and supplies for
making Santas available through Web site or by phone

Personal Expressions

Anna Griffin Inc.
For a store near you, call 888/817-8170.
www.annagriffin.com

Creative Paperclay Company
79 Daily Dr., Suite 101, Camarillo, CA 93010
805/484-6648
www.paperclay.com
Available at local crafts stores or order online

D. Blümchen & Company
P.O. Box 1210-SCC
Ridgewood, NJ 07451-1210
Toll free telephone: 1-866/OLD-XMAS
Fax: 201/652-1759
www.blumchen.com
E-mail: dblumchenandco@aol.com
"The Best of Christmas Past" color catalogue, $3.00

House on the Hill Cookie Molds
House on the Hill, Inc.
P. O. Box 7003, Villa Park, IL 60181
Phone 630/279-4455 Fax 630/279-5544
www.houseonthehill.net
E-mail: info@houseonthehill.net

Old Print Factory
Check local retailers for Old Print Factory products.

Sandy Elliott's Christmas Bazaar
P.O. Box 96, Exeter, NH 03833
603/772-1457
www.sechristmasbazaar.com

Sweet Sensations

Madeleine Santas, *page 152*
Madeleine Pan—Sweet Celebrations; 800/328-6722;
www.sweetc.com.

DIRECTOR, EDITORIAL ADMINISTRATION *Michael L. Maine*
EDITOR-IN-CHIEF *Beverly Rivers*
ART DIRECTOR *Brenda Drake Lesch*
MANAGING EDITOR *Karman Wittry Hotchkiss*
EDITORIAL MANAGER *Ann Blevins*

EDITOR *Dee Foust*
ASSOCIATE ART DIRECTOR *Shawn Roorda*
SENIOR FOOD EDITOR *Lois White*
COPY CHIEF *Mary Heaton*
EDITORIAL ASSISTANT *Cathy Celsi*
CONTRIBUTING GRAPHIC DESIGNER *Kim Hopkins*
CONTRIBUTING COPY EDITOR *David Kirchner*
CONTRIBUTING PROOFREADER *Katherine Nugent*
CONTRIBUTING WRITERS *Kathy Roth Eastman, Allison Engel,*
Judith Stern Friedman, Debra Gibson, Carol McGarvey, Shelley Stewart
PHOTO STYLISTS *Patty Crawford, Sandy Kerman, Pam Knoblauch, Linda Krinn*

VICE PRESIDENT, PUBLISHING DIRECTOR *William R. Reed*

GROUP PUBLISHER *Maureen Ruth*
CONSUMER PRODUCT SENIOR MARKETING MANAGER *Steve Swanson*
CONSUMER PRODUCT MARKETING MANAGER *Karrie Nelson*
BUSINESS DIRECTOR *Christy Light*
BUSINESS MANAGER *Jie Lin*
PRODUCTION MANAGER *Douglas M. Johnston*
BOOK PRODUCTION MANAGERS *Pam Kvitne, Marjorie J. Schenkelberg,*
Rick von Holdt
ASSISTANT TO THE PUBLISHER *Cheryl Eckert*

MEREDITH PUBLISHING GROUP
PUBLISHING GROUP PRESIDENT *Stephen M. Lacy*
MAGAZINE GROUP PRESIDENT *Jerry Kaplan*
CORPORATE SOLUTIONS *Michael Brownstein*
CREATIVE SERVICES *Ellen de Lathouder*
MANUFACTURING *Bruce Heston*
CONSUMER MARKETING *Karla Jeffries*
FINANCE AND ADMINISTRATION *Max Runciman*

CHAIRMAN AND CEO *William T. Kerr*

CHAIRMAN OF THE EXECUTIVE COMMITTEE *E.T. Meredith III*

For editorial questions, please write:
Better Homes and Gardens® Santa Claus Collection, Vol. 5
1716 Locust St., GA 202, Des Moines, IA 50309-3023

A MERRY CHRISTMAS AND HAPPY NEW YEAR

Linda Morrow's collection of glorious antique ornaments graces a time-worn feather tree.

Merry Christmas to All!

Photograph by Ed Gohlich